WITHDRAWN

 TRAINING
DEPARTMENT

D1578968

ALISON HARDINGHAM grew up in Malvern, Worcestershire, and studied psychology at Lady Margaret Hall, Oxford. She trained as a teacher and taught emotionally disturbed children before moving on to educational psychology, including family therapy and assessment of children. She now works as a business psychologist, in the area of management assessment and development. She has particular expertise in the appraisal of an individual's strengths and development needs in relation to his or her chosen career. In recent years she has worked extensively with people in organizations at times of major change. Alison is also the author of *How to Make Successful Decisions* and *How to Get Things Done* (Sheldon 1988 and 1990).

Overcoming Common Problems Series

For a full list of titles please contact
Sheldon Press, Marylebone Road, London NW1 4DU

Beating Job Burnout
DR DONALD SCOTT

Beating the Blues
SUSAN TANNER AND JILLIAN BALL

Being the Boss
STEPHEN FITZSIMON

Birth Over Thirty
SHEILA KITZINGER

Body Language
How to read others' thoughts by their gestures
ALLAN PEASE

Bodypower
DR VERNON COLEMAN

Bodysense
DR VERNON COLEMAN

Calm Down
How to cope with frustration and anger
DR PAUL HAUCK

Changing Course
How to take charge of your career
SUE DYSON AND STEPHEN HOARE

Comfort for Depression
JANET HORWOOD

Complete Public Speaker
GYLES BRANDRETH

Coping Successfully with Your Child's Asthma
DR PAUL CARSON

Coping Successfully with Your Hyperactive Child
DR PAUL CARSON

Coping Successfully with Your Irritable Bowel
ROSEMARY NICOL

Coping with Anxiety and Depression
SHIRLEY TRICKETT

Coping with Blushing
DR ROBERT EDELMANN

Coping with Cot Death
SARAH MURPHY

Coping with Depression and Elation
DR PATRICK McKEON

Coping with Stress
DR GEORGIA WITKIN-LANOIL

Coping with Suicide
DR DONALD SCOTT

Coping with Thrush
CAROLINE CLAYTON

Curing Arthritis – The Drug-Free Way
MARGARET HILLS

Curing Arthritis Diet Book
MARGARET HILLS

Curing Coughs, Colds and Flu – The Drug-Free Way
MARGARET HILLS

Curing Illness – The Drug-Free Way
MARGARET HILLS

Depression
DR PAUL HAUCK

Divorce and Separation
ANGELA WILLANS

Don't Blame Me!
How to stop blaming yourself and other people
TONY GOUGH

The Epilepsy Handbook
SHELAGH McGOVERN

Everything You Need to Know about Adoption
MAGGIE JONES

Everything You Need to Know about Contact Lenses
DR ROBERT YOUNGSON

Everything You Need to Know about Osteoporosis
ROSEMARY NICOL

Overcoming Common Problems Series

Overcoming Common Problems Series

Hysterectomy
SUZIE HAYMAN

Jealousy
DR PAUL HAUCK

Learning from Experience
A woman's guide to getting
older without panic
PATRICIA O'BRIEN

Learning to Live with Multiple Sclerosis
DR ROBERT POVEY, ROBIN DOWIE
AND GILLIAN PRETT

Living Alone – A Woman's Guide
LIZ McNEILL TAYLOR

Living Through Personal Crisis
ANN KAISER STEARNS

Living with Grief
DR TONY LAKE

Living with High Blood Pressure
DR TOM SMITH

Loneliness
DR TONY LAKE

Making Marriage Work
DR PAUL HAUCK

Making the Most of Loving
GILL COX AND SHEILA DAINOW

Making the Most of Yourself
GILL COX AND SHEILA DAINOW

Managing Two Careers
How to survive as a working mother
PATRICIA O'BRIEN

Meeting People is Fun
How to overcome shyness
DR PHYLLIS SHAW

Menopause
RAEWYN MACKENZIE

The Nervous Person's Companion
DR KENNETH HAMBLY

Overcoming Fears and Phobias
DR TONY WHITEHEAD

Overcoming Shyness
A woman's guide
DIANNE DOUBTFIRE

Overcoming Stress
DR VERNON COLEMAN

Overcoming Tension
DR KENNETH HAMBLY

Overcoming Your Nerves
DR TONY LAKE

The Parkinson's Disease Handbook
DR RICHARD GODWIN-AUSTEN

Say When!
Everything a woman needs to know about
alcohol and drinking problems
ROSEMARY KENT

Self-Help for your Arthritis
EDNA PEMBLE

Slay Your Own Dragons
How women can overcome
self-sabotage in love and work
NANCY GOOD

Sleep Like a Dream – The Drug-Free Way
ROSEMARY NICOL

Solving your Personal Problems
PETER HONEY

A Special Child in the Family
Living with your sick or disabled child
DIANA KIMPTON

Think Your Way to Happiness
DR WINDY DRYDEN AND JACK GORDON

Trying to Have a Baby?
Overcoming infertility and child loss
MAGGIE JONES

Why Be Afraid?
How to overcome your fears
DR PAUL HAUCK

Women and Depression
A practical self-help guide
DEIDRE SANDERS

You and Your Varicose Veins
DR PATRICIA GILBERT

Your Arthritic Hip and You
GEORGE TARGET

Your Grandchild and You
ROSEMARY WELLS

Overcoming Common Problems

MAKING CHANGE
WORK FOR YOU

Alison Hardingham

SHELDON PRESS
LONDON

First published in Great Britain 1992
Sheldon Press, SPCK, Marylebone Road, London NW1 4DU

British Library Cataloguing-in-Publication Data
A catalogue record for this book is available from the British Library
ISBN 0–85969–643–X

Photoset by Deltatype Ltd, Ellesmere Port, Cheshire
Printed in Great Britain by Courier International Ltd, East Kilbride

To Jon,
who helped me live it
before he helped me write it

Contents

Introduction

There was a time when the key to organizational success was stability. The businesses and institutions which prospered were the ones which cornered a marketplace or function, established how they were going to capitalize on the opportunities, and 'bedded down' their activities and procedures. A brief entrepreneurial flurry was succeeded by a long bureaucratic march.

Nowadays, however, it is not stable organizations which flourish but quick-footed ones. The notion of cutting a slice of the commercial cake and then spending comfortable and static years digesting it is now totally inappropriate; a better metaphor today is that of trying to take bites out of apples bobbing in a stream. All the pundits are agreed that the pace of change will increase, and that, if it isn't too paradoxical a thought, constant change is now the only certainty.

What are we as individual employees to make of this? For years people looked for the 'right job' and, when they found it, settled down into it. The day's work was a predictable and steady backdrop to life, a source of security, financial and emotional, and a sort of reassuring recurrent melody running through people's life changes. Success for organizations was about stability, control and predictability, so that was what work came to mean. And the more work was ordered and the more workers contributed to a smooth-running system, the more successful they as individuals felt and the more successful they were.

But now stability and predictability are not our goals, but rather warning signs of individual or organizational complacency. 'Settling down into a routine' is now a sign of failure, not an achievement; 'stirring things up' now a responsibility, not a delinquent self-indulgence. Our individual working lives have to mirror – indeed, they determine – the life of the organization we work for: we must be nimble, creative, on the look-out for opportunities, quick to see how things can be improved so that

1

the businesses on which we depend for our livelihood and much of our self-esteem can thrive in the ever-changing environment of the 1990s.

I have spent the last three years observing and intervening in the people aspects of organizational and business life. As a full-time business psychologist and management consultant, I have talked with many individuals caught up in organizational change. I have seen some of those individuals drive change forward, leading the organization to develop in ways the original architects of change never envisaged. I have seen others become depressed and demotivated by the loss of security, stability and predictability in their working lives. I have discussed and debated the issues with individuals from a wide range of organizations, argued heatedly with them about the value of change, the feasibility of improvement, reflected coolly with them about possible outcomes. Through all of this I have observed some patterns of thought, feeling and behaviour emerge, which distinguish those who promote change from those who hide from it. And I have seen things which individuals can do and have done to make change work, and make it stick.

So I have written this book, which is about how we can respond to the enormous shift in emphasis at work from the settled and known to the unpredictable and ambiguous. It is about how we can take advantage of change, rather than suffer it. It is about how we, as individual employees, can be *change agents* – that is, sources of innovation and opportunism in the workplace, not merely passively adaptable but actively driving our organization forward.

The bad news about all of this is that it demands more of us. It demands more energy, more enthusiasm, more ability. The good news is that it gives us immeasurably more. Work can become an opportunity for self-expression, personal as well as professional development, and excitement.

In the pages which follow, you are asked, first of all, to consider how you feel about change and why you feel as you do. For if you feel angry, oppressed or frightened by it, you cannot take advantage of it. We also look at some change agents' stories

– real people who have responded successfully to the oppor-
tunties.

We identify what you can do to be a change agent: where the
opportunities are, what skills you need, and how to exercise
them. And the essential theme running through all of this is that
you don't have to be a boss, director or entrepreneur to bring
about change – and that in fact those few people 'at the top' can't
do it without you.

1

Opportunities, Threats and Betrayals: How Do You Feel About Change?

What is a change agent?

A change agent is someone who sees change primarily as an opportunity, not as a threat, *and* who has the ability and the will to realize the opportunities which change presents.

A change agent may or may not have initiated the change in the first place. This is an important point, because for most of us most of the change we experience is imposed rather than chosen. But that doesn't rob us of the potential to be change agents. Just because someone has told us to do something doesn't mean it's not worth doing, or that we won't enjoy it and make more of it than was ever originally envisaged.

That is the essence of being a change agent. Nothing is fixed in our lives. We try to establish structure, stability, predictability – homes, families, careers. Sometimes we achieve periods where the machinery we have set in motion turns smoothly, effortlessly, without disruption. But we all know that the norm is spokes in the wheel, gravel between the cogs, imposed disturbance, disruption – in short, imposed change.

If we can embrace the change, use the energy and variability it brings in train, to achieve something new and satisfying, then we are change agents.

So you can see from this that, although this book is primarily about change in organizations, being a change agent is in fact a life skill, relevant to all of us. And at many points in the book I will make the links between organizational life and the rest of life. The skills you learn in one are essential in the other. The experiences in both inform each other.

Being a change agent is about being a chess grandmaster, rather than a pawn in someone else's game. It's about capturing the golden balls as they rush towards you and diverting their path to meet your target rather than letting them knock you flat.

The essential qualifications

Can we *all* be change agents? The answer to this question is the same as the answer to most other questions that begin 'can we. . . ?'. It is, of course, 'yes, if we want to enough'.

So what are the basic essentials? What do we need to have in our emotional/psychological kit bag if we aspire to change agency?

We need *self-esteem*, because one of the biggest reasons for resisting or hiding from change is the fear that we won't be up to the challenges it brings. The nature of our job changes; we're frightened we won't be able to learn the new skills. The team we work in changes; we're frightened we won't be able to establish good working relationships with a new set of people.

We need *flexibility*, for obvious reasons: if things are changing we'll need to adapt. If we are a blade of grass, the winds of change will bend but not break us; if we are a twig, we won't be able to channel and use the wind's force and may break.

We also need *curiosity*. Self-esteem and flexibility enable us to cope with change, take it in our stride. But it is curiosity which enables us to welcome it, look for it, hunt it out. If we have curiosity, we are well placed to enjoy change, for it will bring novelty and variety; and we shall find out the answers to some of those 'what if' questions. It is surprising how many of us lose the capacity to be curious – but this loss need only be temporary.

Later in this chapter we shall look at some ways to build self-esteem, flexibility and curiosity (and in this connection you might like to read the section on 'Why Things Don't Get Done' in my book *How to Get Things Done*).

How do you feel about change?

Now it is time for a bit of self-diagnosis. We've investigated what the goal is; let's find out where we're starting from. Complete the following three exercises.*

Self-diagnosis I: wordsearch

Consider the two words *change* and *stability*. Choose the one which appeals to you most. Don't think about it deeply, or analyse why: just pick one.

Many people will in fact have found it very easy to choose one word in preference to the other. For all of us, words are more than just letters in a particular order corresponding to a dictionary definition. They are triggers, keys, links in a chain; they are connected with all sorts of feelings, experiences and thoughts. So two words like 'change' and 'stability' will almost always evoke a complex response in any one of us, a response which may be more or less subconscious, but which has a strong emotional element. And on balance one set of emotional links will be more pleasant, or more exciting, or less frightening, than the other. And that is the basis on which we make our 'choice' between the two words.

Of course, neither word will have entirely positive or negative connotations, and we may find ourselves thinking, for example, 'well, on balance, I'll choose "change", but I do like some stability, I do like to know where I am with people for example . . .'.

Nevertheless, when you ask people to choose between a number of word pairs, the pattern of their choices can be a useful short-cut to understanding what is most important, rewarding, or worrying for them.

Below are 20 pairs of words. Without thinking about why these particular pairs have been chosen, go down the list as quickly as you can and tick the word you prefer.

---

* Self-diagnosis exercises I and III are based on an established personality questionnaire which I use a great deal to help people understand their reactions to change and uncertainty. It is the Myers–Briggs Type Inventory (MBTI) and I can recommend it to anyone working with individuals or organizations at times of change.

A	liquid	O	Victoria	c	picture
B	solid	P	Alanya	d	vision
C	ice	Q	dawn	e	spontaneous
D	water	R	noon	f	systematic
E	rain	S	reliable	g	unruly
F	desert	T	surprising	h	orderly
G	future	U	mercury	i	casual
H	past	V	steel	j	committed
I	rock	W	wall	k	firm
J	gravel	X	screen	l	fluid
H	scheduled	Y	known	m	still
L	unplanned	Z	unknown	n	moving
M	train	a	novel		
N	plane	b	proven		

Give yourself one point for each of the following you have ticked: A, D, E, G, J, L, N, P, Q, T, U, X, Z, a, d, e, g, i, l, n. You will have a score between 0 and 20. Make a note of it.

Self-diagnosis II: storyline

Two stories are told below, each in the first person. Imagine you were in the narrator's shoes as you read them. Then decide, after you have read both, which story you would prefer to be in.

Story 1

I stepped out of the hut into the forest. Light filtered through the leaves, but it was gloomy and I couldn't see a clear trail. I walked carefully through brambles for perhaps ten minutes and then I began to see up ahead the dim purple glow for which I had been searching. I started to run, and suddenly I broke through the trees into a vast clearing. Zan's shining craft was suspended above the carpet of pine needles and I could dimly make out the flims' shapes behind the portholes. I was so happy to have found them, I bounded over the clearing and threw myself up the gangplank. Inside would be what I needed more than anything, what I had already given up so much for; it promised a new beginning, and I could not wait to be near it.

Story 2

I was in a hurry to catch the train. I had managed to put all my business affairs in order that morning but it had taken rather longer than I had envisaged. Anyway, now I was only sixteen hours away from Chris, and from two weeks in Southern Italy. I could picture the farmhouse with its baked mud walls and the lizards waiting to welcome us back; I could picture every room in turn and thought I would spend the train journey recalling all the happy moments I had spent in those rooms. And then the twins would be joining us at the week-end, and we would go fishing off the beach nearby in our battered old dinghy. It promised to be another glorious holiday.

If you chose story 1, give yourself 5 points. If you chose story 2, give yourself 2 points.

Self-diagnosis III: how do you behave?

Now answer these questions, without pondering too deeply.
1. Do you
    (a) rather prefer to do things at the last minute, or
    (b) find doing things at the last minute hard on the nerves?
2. Is it harder for you to adapt to
    (a) routine, or
    (b) constant change?
3. Would you rather
    (a) support the established methods of doing good, or
    (b) analyse what is still wrong and attack unsolved problems?

9

4. When you have a decision to make, do you usually
   (a) make it right away, or
   (b) wait as long as you reasonably can before deciding?
The scoring guidelines for these questions are: 1a 1, 1b 0; 2a 1, 2b 0; 3a 0, 3b 1; 4a 0, 4b 1.

Now add up your scores from all three self-diagnosis quizzes. Your total will be between 2 and 29.

If you scored 10 or below, you are much more naturally inclined towards stability than change.

If you scored 20 or above, you enjoy change and are likely to find it exciting rather than threatening.

Between 10 and 20 or above, your preference is not so clear-cut, but the higher you score, the 'easier' you find change.

Change reactions

Now the first thing to say is, whatever your natural preference with regard to change itself, you will have strengths and limitations when you try to operate as a change agent. Those who are naturally predisposed towards change will probably have an easier time of it emotionally, because they're much less likely to be frightened and depressd by it; but they have their problems when it comes to 'making change stick', which is an essential part of true change agency.

Table 1 shows the strengths and limitations of both ends of the attitude-to-change spectrum. Hopefully the self-diagnosis exercises will help you position yourself on that spectrum; then you can see which natural strengths you have and what the limitations are which you will have to work at to overcome.

In fact we can only succeed as change agents if we learn how to fuse the desire for novelty and the need for stability, if we reconcile our fear of the unknown and our boredom with the known. Change agency challenges us to transcend the sterile conflict between 'what's been good enough so far is good enough now' and 'it must be time for a change'.

Too much stability is death – there's nothing so stable as rigor

Table 1. Attitudes to change, and their strengths and limitations

I need stability		I need change	
STRENGTHS	LIMITATIONS	STRENGTHS	LIMITATIONS
• Will work hard to establish new systems and structures.	• May waste energy resisting or arguing against inevitable change.	• Will find change energizing; will be at the forefront of introducing it.	• May be bored by the need to 'bed the change in'.
• Will see the real disadvantages and obstacles to change.	• May be slow to see the real opportunities change brings.	• Will quickly see how things could be different and better.	• May overlook the value of the old; may 'reinvent the wheel'.
• Will work to ensure that the benefits of the old are preserved in the new.	• Will often feel uncomfortable, even frightened, at times of change.	• Will feel free of stress and excited at times of change.	• May engage in 'change for change's sake'.
• Will work out and follow through the implications of the change; will make sure the change is completed.	• May make others feel anxious about change.	• Will be able to enthuse others for change.	• May be impatient with people who don't want to change.

mortis. And yet, paradoxically, too much change is decay – when the fabric of life begins to disintegrate, to alter, to shift and flux.

Life and hope are to be found in the fusion of change and sameness, in getting the balance right, in changing the right things and keeping other things the same.

That is the proper territory of the change agent.

It is just as much the responsibility of the change agent to make links between the future and the past as it is to break chains: for if there are no links, the future cannot be understood, the change has no roots and it will not grow.

So whether you scored 2 or 29 in the self-diagnosis exercises or somewhere in between, you will have some useful resources to draw on in the journey towards change agency as well as some blocks to overcome.

Childhood and change

Before considering how you can make best use of your strengths and overcome your limitations, wherever you sit on the attitude-to-change spectrum, it's worth pausing to reflect on where our 'natural' preferences with regard to change come from.

Like most of our strong underlying characteristics, they have their roots in childhood experiences. Children from very structured and controlling families, where the parents believe that the best thing they can do for their sons and daughters is to give them stability, will not have had much practice flexing and bending in the winds of change. Their attitude to change may be largely a fear of the unknown.

Children from families who move around a lot, who have a more haphazard and unpredictable day-to-day lifestyle, are used to change. They may actually find that the thought of routine and predictability makes them anxious.

On the other hand, sometimes it is exactly these children, whose childhood has been turbulent, who crave structure and stability later in life.

You might like to reflect on your experiences of change and stability in your own childhood. You may find there the key to how you feel about them now. Anything which helps you understand why you feel the way you do gives you more control over the way you feel.

Why do we fear change?

Whatever your attitude to change, before looking at how you can make the most of your strengths and overcome your weaknesses, let's consider for a moment where our universal fear of change comes from.

In one sense, change is the most normal and enduring aspect of all our lives. No two days are the same; in fact, no two minutes are the same. This is true for the physical world of objects just as it is true for our psychological and emotional worlds. The molecules which constitute the desk on which I'm resting, the chair on which you're sitting, are moving, changing their positions, rearranging themselves, all the time.

Stability is an illusion. But it appears to be a very necessary illusion for all of us. Parents work hard to provide 'stable backgrounds' for their children; we all try to establish 'stable relationships'; we talk and think about some of the most comfortable periods of our lives as times when 'life just went on as usual, nothing much happened'.

In fact, we human beings are outstanding as a species for our ability to impose order on an unstructured and constantly changing world. We build, we categorize, we control; we make the environment round us more fixed, more predictable.

All of this suggests that the stability-change dimension will always be a very significant one for all of us. We know or sense the changeability of everything, and we also know or sense that our survival depends on our managing that changeability into some kind of order. Otherwise all our energies and efforts are used up continuously adapting, and there are no resources left to grow, think, create, plan. You can see this most clearly in a child's development: if she has 'background stability' – a predictable home environment, parents who behave consistently towards her over a long period of time – then she is free to

13

develop, to learn, to make friends, and she will grow up. If she is brought up in a turbulent environment, whilst she may cope with it well, large areas of her emotional, psychological and sometimes even physical growing up will be neglected, and she will need to do that growing up later, when she is already chronologically adult.

Also, whilst knowing that some kind of stability is so important to our survival and growth as human beings, we also know that all stability is an illusion. And too much change, too fast, threatens to shatter the illusion, and frightens us.

What is the nature of that fear? Think yourself back to a time of change in your life. It might have been change of job, change of home, change in your family structure. Leaving home/marrying/having children/divorcing are typical major changes for many of us.

Think about the kind of apprehension you experienced at the time. It probably had some or all of these components.

Fear of loss. At times of change, we rarely have certainty about the good things the change will bring. So we think about the good things we have which the change will take away. Children leaving home will often be very apprehensive about losing everyday emotional support from their parents.

Fear of challenge. We recognize that the change will make new demands on us, and we worry that we won't have the skills or qualities to satisfy those demands. This is often a major source of apprehension for people changing jobs.

Fear of chaos. As we have already said, we work so hard to bring order into our lives. Major changes threaten that order, and make us wonder if everything is going to go out of control permanently.

Fear of losing control. This is linked with fear of chaos. We reassure ourselves we are masters, or mistresses, of our own destiny by controlling things and events – and people – around us. Change threatens to push us off balance and then we fear ending up being controlled. Contributing to this fear is the feeling that we won't know the rules so well in the changed state. It will be, literally, a different 'ball game'.

However high or low you scored in the self-diagnosis quizzes, you will have some elements of these fears. So don't expect ever to find change painless; but feel the fear and do it anyway!

Let's look more closely now at the resources you will need to overcome the fear.

Getting ready for change

I said, at the start of this chapter, that what you need to be a change agent is self-esteem, flexibility and curiosity. Wherever you are on the attitude-to-change spectrum, you are going to need large doses of all three. So how can you increase your stocks?

Self-esteem

There are two kinds of self-esteem: general and specific. The general kind is to do with how comfortable you feel with yourself, to what extent you are sure you are worth something alongside other people, your sense of your own value. It is fundamental to sane, healthy living, but you need even more of it than the basic minimum to be an effective change agent.

The specific kind of self-esteem is to do with particular activities or contacts. For example, many individuals I have met during the course of my work have a high sense of self-worth in their work, often bolstered by symbols of status and recognition from others, but in their domestic life they feel inferior to others and doubt their value or effectiveness as spouses and parents. Some people may have very high self-esteem in just one narrow area – a particular leisure pursuit or technical skill, for example – and much lower self-esteem everywhere else.

Too much specific self-esteem attached to a particular activity or context can be a trap if it isn't matched by a high level of general self-esteem. For if someone threatens to take away the only activity that you feel valued for, you will either become deeply depressed or fight tooth and nail to retain it.

I came across a senior personnel manager in one of my consultancy assignments, who was a very good example of this.

15

Her skill and expertise were in industrial relations – she had an excellent track record in negotiating tough pay deals with trade unions without incurring even the threat of strike action. In many other work and domestic situations she was rather ineffectual, but in industrial relations she was supremely confident and it showed. When the organization wanted to move away from unionization towards responsible autonomous working teams, with managers and shop floor working out for themselves the terms and conditions of the whole team, this personnel manager was completely lost. She could not see a role for herself in the new-look organization (although in fact she could have been a very useful internal consultant to the teams). She fought the changes, unsuccessfully (although she did delay a large number of initiatives), and then, unwillingly, took early retirement. Her self-esteem was too specific to allow her to move with the path of change.

Jot down quickly all the things you do or people you spend time with where you feel valued. It will give you a rough and ready guide to how specific (and therefore limiting) your self-esteem is.

Have you listed a wide range, covering lots of different aspects of your life, or is everything focused on one or two people or one area of your life?

What can we do to build up our levels of general self-esteem? Here are some practical suggestions: they will cover things you can do in your personal life as well as things to do in the work context – remember that those two parts of your life are resources for each other.

- Spend as much time as possible with people who value you and who show it.
- Spend as little time as possible with people who don't value you, or who accidentally put you down or make you feel bad about yourself in other ways. It is often difficult in the work context to exert control over who you spend your time with; and life is particularly tough for those many individuals who have bosses who fail to make them feel valued. If you have to

work close to people who are 'vexatious to the spirit' (to quote from Desiderata), then make sure in your own time you make up for it. Carry your good friends and your close family around with you in your head at work; tune in to their opinion of you when your boss is giving you a hard time.

- Learn a new skill; find out about a new subject area.
- Keep a journal of your successes – many of us remember only our failures.
- Find out what energizes you and give yourself regular doses of it: it could be music, physical exercise, a particular kind of task accomplishment – it could be anything!

Flexibility

Flexibility is about developing new behaviours and patterns, about surprising yourself and other peope, about extending your limits as a person.

It's easy to recognize inflexibility in others – and we see it far too often. We all know the individual who always denigrates new ideas, for example; we all know the individual who can be relied on to remind us about practicalities. But it's just as easy to overlook inflexibility in ourselves as it is to spot it in others. We invariably overestimate our own flexibility. It's a classic psychological illusion that we respond differently and appropriately and in a wide range of ways. It belongs in the self delusional junkheap, along with

'I'm always reasonable in arguments'
'I never lose my sense of humour/sense of perspective/temper'
'I can always see the other person's point of view'

In fact, we could all benefit from more flexibility. Think about someone you always get into arguments with. Imagine how else you could respond to his infuriating remarks. Brainstorm some ideas. You could laugh/offer him a biscuit/start talking about something completely different/imagine him standing on his head. There are so many ways we could respond, and yet we select again and again from a tiny range of possibilities.

If it would be beneficial for everyone to develop more flexibility, it's absolutely essential for change agents to do so. But how? Here are some tips.

- Practise the gentle art and powerful technique of reframing (see Chapter 2, 'Decision Frames', in my book *How to Make Successful Decisions*). The key to responding to a situation differently is very often *seeing* it differently, giving it a different meaning, in the first place. You can see another road-user's bad driving as a monumental lack of courtesy, or as an opportunity for you to demonstrate your driving skill. You can see your colleague's objections to your new plan as jealous obstructionism or as a concern that the plan should be absolutely right before being implemented. You will respond totally differently, depending on which frame you use.
- Learn as much about your innate preferences and biases as you can. Concentrate on not letting them always determine how you behave.
- Make it your aim to surprise someone at least once a week – by the way you respond to a task, a situation or a suggestion.
- Watch out for telltale signs from the people around you that you are behaving in an utterly predictable way. These signs may range from having their answer ready before you've even started to speak (you can usually read this in someone's eyes –it's the point at which they stop listening to you and start 'waiting to speak') to falling asleep when they're with you.
- Study people whom you consider to be very different from you. How are they different? Learn from them. Often, if you find yourself saying about someone 'I could never be like that', they are just the person you could learn from to enhance your flexibility.
- When you engage in a task or activity, set yourself two kinds of goal. The first is *what* you will achieve, the second is *how* you will achieve it. Challenge yourself to achieve things in different ways. For example, you might want to make sure a meeting you were chairing finished on time. For one meeting, you might set yourself the goal of achieving it through rigorous

18

timekeeping; for another, you might set yourself the goal of achieving it without mentioning the time once but managing the flow of the meeting. This practice has another very strong benefit. It scotches the notion that there is only one 'right' or 'best' way to do things and it encourages you to experience and therefore believe that there are always many good ways of getting to the same endpoint. This in itself builds flexibility.

Curiosity

Why do we stop being curious? Why does it often take the presence of children to reawaken curiosity in us? I suppose we start being mainly interested in preserving what *is* there, and that takes up so much time that there's little left for investigating what *might be* there. Also, when change is suggested, sometimes the anxiety arrives so quickly that it blocks out the curiosity we might have felt. In fact, fear and curiosity are pretty incompatible, for fear focuses us on putting up the defences and it's well-nigh impossible to see out of a shuttered fortress.

So the suggestions here for increasing our curiosity have as much to do with holding back the emotions and reactions which impede our natural curiosity as they do with specifically cultivating more curiosity.

- Replace the 'but' approach with the 'and' approach. Here's a piece of dialogue to illustrate:

   'We're going to move the Admin Department up to the first floor.'
   'But what about the computer system? We've only just got it sorted out where it is.'

Did you hear the barriers go up with the 'But'? And the speaker will now be locked *into* objecting, *out of* investigating. Contrast:

   'We're going to move the Admin Department up to the first floor.'

'And what plans have you got for the computer system?'

Now the speaker is in investigative mode: he isn't overlooking an important issue, but neither is he getting locked into sterile confrontation.

- Give 'why' questions a high priority in your thinking. Always try to understand as much as you can. Remember, if the planned change is a bad one, you'll be able to argue against it even more effectively for having investigated first. Why has it been proposed, and why now? As soon as you can after you have reacted in terms of how the change will affect you, put yourself in other people's shoes and explore how it will affect them.

- Play with ideas. Practise imagining all sorts of ways in which things could be different when you know things are in fact likely to stay the same. Exercise your curiosity in a safe environment.

- Exercise your curiosity by finding things out. Maybe there are aspects of the organization you work in that you have never grasped. Find out about them. Take one of the financial people out to lunch and ask her to explain the accounting system; spend time with the technical specialists and find out exactly what they do.

- Identify inquisitive people. Spend time with them. Curiosity can be 'caught'.

- Build your self-esteem. The more you have, the freer you'll be to be curious.

- Think about the proportion of questions you ask to statements you make. Think about opportunities you've missed, things you could have found out about but didn't ask enough questions. Ask more. Always ask yourself what it would be interesting or important to know.

2

Jabberwocky and Jetsam: Developing Your Creativity

This chapter is about how to make the most of the chances you get to determine the nature and course of a change. It's about having ideas, imagining how things could be different, seeing where and how things can be moved. It's about being the source of change. It's about *creativity*.

Chambers English Dictionary defines the verb 'create' as follows:

> to bring into being or form out of nothing; to bring into being by force of imagination; to make, produce, or form; to design; to invest with a new form, office or character; to institute; to be the first to act (a part).

Creativity is highly prized, and creative people – poets, artists, musicians, writers – are often talked about as if they were a race apart.

In fact, I firmly believe that every one of us is naturally creative. It is part of our genetic inheritance that we make things; we are unique among all species in the extent of our making. And not only do we 'bring into being or form' things which are functional (such as buildings, cars, televisions), but we also create objects and experiences of beauty which do nothing other than add to the interest and complexity of the natural world.

When you reflect on all this, you can hardly escape the conclusion that to be human is to create.

Look around you, and you'll see evidence of creativity everywhere. It's not just in the Louvre or the Albert Hall; it's in the VW Beetle whose owner has painted it pink with yellow spots; it's in the topiary butterfly in a neighbour's garden; it's in cooking, in putting a home together, in playing with children, in handwritten signatures, in jokes.

Why, then, do so many of us say 'I'm not very creative'? Why do organizations and the individuals within them often become monuments to repetitiveness? Why is such a big fuss made about the need to encourage employees to have ideas and to have special and very highly paid 'ideas' jobs like 'creative director' or 'head of future strategy', when in fact organizations are already stuffed full of creative people – that is, ordinary people?

There are three answers to these questions. The first is to do with the fact that we don't recognize certain types of creativity, in ourselves or in other people. We shut out much that is creative, or fail to see its value, because of some stereotyped notions we have of what creativity is. The second is to do with the many blocks to our natural creativity. The third is to do with the particular blocks to creativity which organizations create. Let's think about each of these answers in turn, and what can be done about them.

Different kinds of creativity

Before you decide you're not a creative person, reflect on all the different ways there are of being creative. The key thing, thinking back to the dictionary definition, is to bring something into being. (That's why, for many of us, having our children represents for us the pinnacle of our creativity. But of course, in a work context, 'creativity' usually implies mental rather than physical creativity.)

Pure or 'true' creativity

When God created heaven and earth out of absolute nothingness, that, of course, was the epitome of creativity. And for many of us the Creation is the implicit reference point when thinking of creativity. The truly creative person, we think, has ideas out of nowhere, has sudden 'flashes of inspiration', takes a blank sheet of paper and turns it into a picture, a poem, a new insight.

In fact, I doubt that much creativity of the pure kind happens.

After all, our minds, lives and environments are definitely nothing like blank sheets of paper, more like dense columns of newsprint, and so if we did want to create something out of the void we'd have to find the void first. More often, we create something out of something else that is already there.

Linking creativity

Many new ideas and new ways forward are generated by someone making a connection between two existing practices, concepts, objects or whatever, which hasn't been made before. Mythological beasts are the classic examples of linking creativity: a griffin, for example, is an imaginary animal with a lion's body and an eagle's beak and wings; no element of the griffin is newly created, but the link is new, and the griffin has a force and magic which is more than the sum of its parts. This is the power of linking creativity.

When you create a new team or working partnership, you are using linking creativity. Some people have the knack of creating highly effective project teams by choosing the right mix of individuals, bearing in mind the skills they have to offer. There is an entire body of psychological theory concerning the formation of teams which add up to more than the sum of their parts, and 'Belbin's Team Roles Inventory' is a questionnaire which is widely used in helping people discover the particular strengths they can bring to teamwork, thus facilitating the process of effective team building.

One project for which I had to select the team benefited enormously from pairing an undoubtedly charismatic but rather volatile personality with a steady individual who paid a lot of attention both to the detail of the task and to the feelings of others. This team ran a series of workshops together, and the participants reported afterwards that they had been excited and enthused and *also*, very importantly, reassured about their own level of competence throughout the workshops.

Linking creativity is what you're using when you see patterns which help you understand what's really going on. You are using linking creativity when you identify political alliances between

23

people at the office ('Jim will always side with Stephanie, and always undermine Jack'), when you see connections between separate projects ('If we had some of the same team on that development project as we've got on the new marketing strategy, we'd be sure of reflecting our most current thinking in our public relations campaign'), when you see how an established method, tool or technique could be used in a new context ('I'm sure we could use our own admin database package as the basis for the record system in that proposal we're making to the client').

Organizations talk a lot about 'synergy' nowadays. This is basically using linking creativity to enhance organizational effectiveness and/or efficiency. You create synergy by spotting where lessons learned in one part of the organization could benefit another part, and by setting up communication channels between the two parts. You create synergy by spotting where two initiatives, if they were combined, would move much further forward than either would alone. For example, if you link assessment of people with design of training, you get assessment which is much more focused and clearly useful, you get people who understand that there's something in assessment for them and commit to it more, and you get training which meets clearly identified needs.

Many people I know and work with, who would hotly deny being 'creative' in any sense, practise linking creativity, day in day out, as a matter of course. They are organizational fixers, and they are invaluable. So recognize your linking creativity and take pride in it.

Reconciling or transformational creativity

Reconciling or transformational creativity is related to linking creativity but it goes a bit further. Here's an example of it in action.

A business school I worked with recently had an academic department headed by a director of studies, and a commercial department headed by a director of marketing. The academic department was responsible for the design and delivery of programmes, the commercial department for selling the programmes to business.

24

The school was not doing very well at the end of the 1980s. Its programmes rarely ran at full strength; the number of its permanent staff had had to be cut; there was not much innovation in programme design. At every meeting the head of the school held with his directors of studies and marketing, they blamed each other for the problems. One would claim: 'You weren't designing the programmes the clients want, and your teaching is out of date and uninspired.' The other would counter with: 'You aren't putting enough effort into marketing, and you don't understand how to sell our programmes effectively.'

The head of the school was in despair. But out of his desperation sprang an extremely neat piece of transformational creativity. He abandoned the departmental structure of the school, made both directors responsible for programme design *and* marketing but in different subject areas, and organized the people below them similarly. Everyone above a certain level had responsibility for design, marketing, and delivery of a specific programme range. Within months, the programme portfolio of the school had become more appropriate to client needs, uptake of courses by businesses had increased substantially, and, just as importantly, no more time was wasted trying to resolve sterile conflicts between the academics and the marketeers.

Transformational creativity is about using the energy which is generated by conflict to create an innovative solution. The conflict can be between people, between goals, between ideas. It requires us to believe that there is a solution which will satisfy both parties in the conflict, that one doesn't have to be sacrificed for the other. It requires us to focus so hard on the clash that the reconciliation emerges.

Craziness

Of course, *absolute* craziness is not creativity. It is destructive, not constructive.

But since craziness is about losing touch with reality – that is, what is here and now – it can be a means of generating new ideas, of changing things, of seeing things in a different light.

Craziness is about breaking rules because you haven't even

noticed they're there. A bit of craziness can help you break free of all the normal constraints and be creative.

You can link craziness with humour and playfulness in thinking about creativity. Sometimes giving people the time and space to be a bit crazy is exactly what gets them out of the rut and into being more creative.

I know a very adept change agent who works within a traditional, very large, very bureaucratic – and incidentally very commercially troubled – manufacturing company. She uses craziness to free people from their ideas-killing seriousness in the work context. Her behaviour doesn't fit at all with what one would expect from a senior executive in one of the UK's most established manufacturers. I have seen her take groups of people along disused railway tracks to draw anything they see that reminds them of work; I have seen her ask everyone in a meeting to shut their eyes and put their hands up if they disagree with what the last speaker has just said.

I have also seen many sterile unproductive meetings turn into lively sessions full of ideas – and what's turned them is the 'meetings clown' who makes a joke, puts a ridiculous perspective on something, uses a bit of craziness. (Most organizations are preoccupied with keeping meetings clowns in order and it's true that if they dominate too much they can waste a lot of time; but what's the point of a very efficient sober meeting if nothing changes as a consequence?)

Extending or building creativity

People who are skilled at extending or building creativity almost always think of themselves as 'uncreative'. Yet without them, most ideas would be stillborn: they pick up the bit of creativity defined in the dictionary as 'to . . . produce, or form; to invest with a new form. . . ; to institute'. Because they give other people's ideas shape and form, they prevent them from just floating around in the ether and make sure they have impact.

I have a colleague whose building creativity is a major part of what he gives to his employing organization. He tracks down people he recognizes to be creative – that is, people who have

26

new ideas – and then he works with them to make their ideas count. He tests out how the ideas would be viewed in the wider organization; he works out what their implementation would mean in practice. He maps out a timescale for their introduction; he challenges them when he senses they would not fit.

But in fact it would be wrong to imply that people are *either* good at building creativity *or* good at the other, more 'sparky' sorts. People can be good at both. One of the most useful things you can do for people who have had an idea is to ask them something about it which will take their thinking further. This is building creativity, and we can all do it.

However, it's important to do it in a way which doesn't put their idea down. It happened to me when I was talking with a friend about the idea for this book. He said, out of genuine interest and curiosity: 'What's your message? What are you wanting to say in the book?' This question helped me get much clearer about who I was writing for and why. It contributed to the creation of this book. It is a good example of building creativity.

Blocks to our natural creativity

The basic theme of the previous section was that you're already a good deal more creative than you probably realize. However, there are many blocks to your natural creativity, and many of them are not easily overcome.

- *Fear*. If we are frightened, we cannot be creative. Fear makes us defend and protect, close up the windows, pull up the drawbridge; it turns us in on ourselves. Creativity requires us to be looking out, experimenting, risking.
- *Self-consciousness*. You can never be sure what people will think of your creations. They might laugh, they might faint, they might criticize, they might ignore. So if you're too preoccupied with other people's reactions, it will stunt your creativity.
- *Depression*. Depression is about believing that you can't change anything, that things are bad and always will be.

Depression is about passivity. In many ways, it is the opposite of creativity.

- *Obsessions*. You generally need some emotional and mental balance to be creative. (I know you will point to all those crazy artists, completely unbalanced, madly in love or despair or delusion, but they are not very helpful role models in learning about the practice of what I would call 'normal' creativity.) So if you are obsessed with some narrow aspect of your life, such as your children's upbringing or your latest love affair, creativity in most areas of your life is likely to be blocked. As with fear, you'll be too focused and closed. Creativity needs air to breathe.

- *Reluctance to commit*. Creativity is about commitment. We speak of 'committing ourselves to paper': the picture is very apt. We have to invest in our ideas, plans and suggestions to bring them out into the open, to let them exist in some shape or form. So, paradoxically, some people's creativity is blocked because they have too many ideas and they can't commit to any of them.

Don't be too depressed: there are ways round and over these obstacles! But before we look at them, let's consider the particular blockages which organizations throw in the path of anyone who wants to be creative in their midst (and this despite affirming that they want their people to be innovative and sending them on 'creative problem-solving' courses!).

- *Hierarchy*. Most organizations are hierarchical, to a greater or lesser extent. And what hierarchies are about is controlling the range of actions people in different organizations can take. So, ultimately, hierarchy is inimical to creativity – the essence of creativity is freedom, and the essence of hierarchy is restriction. (On a more prosaic level, I have heard people at the bottom of the hierarchy – with lots of natural creativity, as demonstrated by their wit, humour and interesting leisure activities – say 'I'm not paid enough to be creative'.)

- *Institutionalized fear*. Organizations generate their own kinds of fear. In the current economic climate, fear of losing your job is quite universal. Then there is fear of not fitting in, fear of making a 'career-limiting' mistake, fear of humiliation (yes, the school of 'management by humiliation' is still alive and kicking, unfortunately). It's hardly surprising that creativity fails to flourish when these kinds of fear are added to all the general fears people have about change.

- *Too much seriousness*. Work is a serious matter – or at least that's what we're led to believe. We wear grey suits to work, we conduct meetings in solemn tones, we take ourselves so seriously. The risk is that we drive out the playfulness from which ideas spring. I think you can probably measure the creative health of an organization with a laughometer.

- *Routine*. It's a sad but inescapable fact of organizational life that there are lots of routine things to be done. Organizations need to be predictable to their markets; they need routine internally to support this. The problem is that people get into the routine 'mind-set': because they are so often asked to do the same thing over and over again, work becomes something to be survived rather than something actively to be *done*.

- *Punishment of creativity*. This is surprising, given that most people now accept that creativity is an essential prerequisite to organizational survival. The problem is that organizations want to have their cake and eat it – they want to have creativity on their terms; they want to control it. One of the consequences is that creativity which is perceived to be 'out of line' is severely punished. Two examples will illustrate this, one general, one personal.

Recent research suggests that when organizations contract, it tends to be the people who 'don't fit' who are made redundant. There is no evidence that those people are any less good at the job, and in fact there is some significant evidence to the contrary; but they are often people who have challenged the status quo and tried to bring about changes.

I used to work for a small company, one of whose major *products* was supposed to be creativity. We hired out consultants to bureaucratic, stultified organizations and these con-

29

sultants were often asked to revitalize the organization, design new and more nimble systems, get things moving. Inside the consultancy, however, creativity was anything but nurtured. One consultant, for example, brought in a kettle and tea-making equipment because he didn't enjoy the machine coffee the company provided. Not very creative, but too creative for the company. He was strongly rebuked because of the risk of his spilling tea on his carpet! We were not allowed to rearrange the office furniture, not even allowed to move our desks by a few inches. This company is now in deep trouble. I have no doubt that its controlling and ultimately punishing approach to creativity inside the company starved it of the creativity it needed to sell to its clients. Innovative people with plenty of initiative either left or used their creativity outside office hours. Unfortunately, you still see bosses who effectively punish their subordinates for having good ideas because they believe it threatens their own position.

With all these blocks to our creativity, you may be beginning to think that it's a miracle that anyone ever gets a new idea or does something different. What can be done to clear these blocks? There are two good ways forward, and you can try either or both depending on the situation and on your feelings about it.

The first way is to investigate very thoroughly the particular situation in which you want to be creative and in which you feel blocked. Ask yourself the question: 'What would have to change for me to be creative here?' List everything you can think of! This is a *creativity block analysis* (CBA, as opposed to ABC: now that's creative to start with, using the alphabet backwards).

Here's the CBA a colleague of mine produced when she was asked to write the copy for a marketing leaflet on one of her firm's new products. (It was the first time she'd written copy, by the way.)

- My skill level: I don't feel I know enough about doing this.
- Time availability: this is something I'm going to need to spend

some stretches of time thinking about and at the moment I'm rushing about, juggling 10 balls in the air.
- The way Alistair manages me: the thought of him tearing my first draft to pieces puts me right off even starting.

Having done this, she then set about removing the blocks. The first and third she removed with a plan that was a stroke of creativity in its own right – in fact, one of linking creativity. She asked Alistair to spend an hour with her talking about the approach to the leaflet – he had considerable experience of writing this kind of copy. The synergy this piece of creativity brought about meant that the hour served a double purpose: my colleague increased her skill level at the same time as changing the way Alistair managed the task. He was co-author rather than harsh critic. The second block to her creativity – time – she removed by negotiating a half-day at home to work on the leaflet, removed from all interruptions.

The really useful thing about CBA is that it gets us thinking about creativity as if it were not some Holy Grail, some magic spiritual state that can only be reached if we recite 'Kubla Khan' backwards into the setting sun one thousand times, but something we can work towards practically.

The second approach is to do some general work on the important aspects of your frame of mind. Clearly, if you are seriously depressed or in genuine fear, you will have to seek outside help to deal with the problem, and becoming more creative is likely to be fairly low on your list of priorities anyway. But the milder forms of fear, self-consciousness, depression, obsession and reluctance to commit are things we can do something about. These are the kinds of things we can do:

- *Physical activity*. Running, swimming, playing tennis – whatever form of physical exercise you enjoy – is a very good way to regain your equilibrium and release your creativity.
- *Meditation*. There is insufficient space to do justice here to this vital form of mental exercise, but meditation on what you can do (as opposed to rumination on what you can't), visioning of

how things could be different, reflection on images and experiences which give you pleasure and peace – all this kind of mental activity releases creativity.

- *Laughter*. Find something or someone who makes you laugh: this always takes you 'out of yourself' and into a more creative space.
- *Action*. Just write something, go somewhere, do something – the first step to *creating* is to *act*. Read books you enjoy, watch good films, talk with good friends: the more good experiences you have inside you, the more likely something good is to come out of you.

But what do you do if the organization, your boss, the environment hems you in, oppresses you, blocks your creativity at every turn and stops you exercising, laughing, acting and enjoying? This is a big enough topic to deserve looking at in the next chapter.

3

Leverage: How to Make Large Changes From Small Beginnings

Imagine the kind of environment which would release your creativity, make you feel like taking the initiative – in short, encourage you to be a change agent. To help you imagine, let me describe my ideal.

I am in an open and very light place, where there is much beauty within sight. Some of it is natural beauty – trees, running water, birds – some of it is the sort of paintings, interesting furnishings and music which I like. I have a quiet space where I can sit comfortably and write; I don't have to look at the beauty; but I know it is there and I can lift my eyes and take in some of it whenever I choose.

Nearby there are novels, works of reference, today's newspapers; I can dip into these if I feel like it. There are all the materials I need at hand, which in my case don't amount to much – endless supplies of good white paper, a smooth-flowing pen, pencils, a rubber.

It is quiet, but not deathly so; I can hear the murmur of other people talking and working; but the room is so arranged that I can easily switch off from the background hum and focus on my own thoughts.

I can make myself a cup of tea or coffee, eat a piece of fruit or a sandwich whenever I want to. There is space for me to walk around. There is no telephone, and people look to see if I am in the middle of writing or thinking before they come to talk to me.

I know I am valued here, and trusted. I have people who I would count as good friends nearby; sometimes I work with them. I have no doubt that my work matters to the people around me – they are always interested in what is going well, what badly. They can be relied on for an objective opinion or to join in a discussion with enthusiasm and knowledge.

When I walk into this working place, I feel very comfortable and peaceful. I also feel mildly excited at the things I have planned for the day. I am greeted with smiles, and people ask about my family.

Is this similar to what you would imagine? Is this an environment where you too could have ideas, make things happen?

Let me describe an environment which would have the opposite effect for me, which would render me practically incapable of good, innovative work.

I am sitting somewhere with no light from outside. The walls are of an indeterminate colour and rather dirty. There is a slightly unpleasant smell which I catch scent of intermittently. There isn't a great deal of space: I am in a small, box-shaped room.

I share this room with someone I don't get on with very well. There's no active animosity, but I really don't have much in common with her and communication on any subject is something of a strain.

The telephone rings incessantly. My room-mate and I never know who the call is for, so there is the continuous distraction of deciding whether to pick it up or not. Every so often, someone comes into the room and demands that something be done immediately.

There are many small irritations. The pencils are blunt and the pencil sharpener doesn't work properly. I have to write on very poor-quality paper: ink spreads; the paper breaks if you try to rub out pencil.

Coffee is served from a trolley at 11 a.m., tea at 3 p.m. Both are made with powdered milk. The coffee is always too strong.

I'm not sure of my ground with the other people around. The atmosphere is uneasy and tense. When I make mistakes, people are quick to point the finger. I can never be sure of support for my ideas.

This sounds like a nightmare for anyone who is interested in producing creative work. Yet it is much closer to the reality many of us work in than the picture I painted first.

Let's abstract from these two pictures the themes and turn them into a creativity health-check for your organization.

CREATIVITY-PROMOTING	CREATIVITY-STIFLING
Space	Restriction
Freedom and flexibility	Control and rigidity
Food for thought	Sterile
Valuing	Critical
Generous	Penny-pinching
Support	Isolation
Choice	Imposition
Peace	Interruption

How does your organization fare on the creativity health-check? If it's right over in the creativity-stifling box, with no real prospect of change, you probably ought to leave.

But if it has some periods, some functions, some relationships which are creativity-promoting, there is a lot you can do to change the creativity-stifling bits or to bring about change even despite them.

The key is to analyse the points of interaction between you as an individual and the organization, and to identify those points at which you can have most impact.

You can draw pictures of the relative power of the organization as a whole and of a single individual within it that looks like figures 1 and 2 on page 36.

If the individual and the organization are 'just sitting there', as it were, then there's absolutely no contest: the organization has more weight, more power, every time (see figure 1).

But there are some points of interaction between individual and organization which shift the balance. These are leverage points for change. If you learn to recognize the leverage points in your organization, and use them, you will begin to bring about

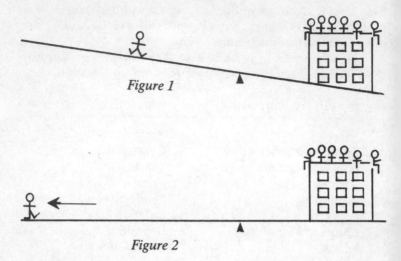

Figure 1

Figure 2

change in spite of that huge organizational inertia which is operating against you (as in figure 2).

Where can we find these leverage points, then?

Contacts with colleagues

Because of the ripple effect of interpersonal behaviour – that is to say, if I behave towards you in a certain way, the chances are you'll behave in a way influenced by that with two or more other people, who will then behave accordingly with five or more other people each, and so on – contact with colleagues is definitely a leverage point for change. In fact, you can see it working as leverage for negative change every day of the week when the whole room full of people will turn sour and unproductive, just because one individual has had a contretemps with another. Every contact with a colleague is an opportunity either to confirm the organization's existing values and *modus operandi* or to change them in the direction of something better.

Contacts with the boss

For many of us, the boss is our primary route of access to the decision-makers. So contact with him or her definitely has potential for leverage. In fact, as we all know only too well, realizing that potential is fraught with difficulty caused by the hierarchical relationship. That is why books have been written and many courses taught on 'how to manage your boss'.

The only point I want to make on this topic is: never underestimate the importance of your boss as a leverage point, even if to you he or she appears lazy, shortsighted and cowardly. If you give up on developing a relationship with him or her which enables you to use the leverage, you have certainly lost out. I have seen many people who were tempted into trying to bypass, take on, or even ignore their bosses; not one brought about the kind of change they were looking for. The way the vast majority of organizations still work means that it is still an organizational taboo for a subordinate to topple a boss – even temporarily, even on a well-defined issue. Getting the boss on your side on something which matters to you is well worth the effort.

Contacts with customers

If you have the opportunity for direct contact with the people who buy (directly or indirectly) your organization's services or products, then you have one of the best leverage points of all. All organizations are now recognizing how vital to their survival it is to listen to their customers, and you are an access point to the customer. Things that you learn from customers, practices that you establish with them, can have huge reverberations on the organization as a whole. I know of one service organization where a newly appointed junior manager was desperately trying to raise the standard of proposal production. (Proposals are documents which go out to prospective clients stating what you can offer them and how much it will cost. On the basis of the proposal and perhaps a meeting or two, the client will decide who to buy from.) This junior manager had relatively little impact until a prospective client told her that the typing errors and unprofessional layout in the organization's recent proposal had been instrumental in the client's decision to buy from someone else. The junior manager used this feedback to create a sense of urgency around proposal production, and this was one of the key driving forces behind the firm's decision to upgrade its word-processing system.

Leadership opportunities

When you get the chance to lead a team, you have a double leverage point. Firstly, you have an opportunity to head a piece of the organization in a way largely determined by you. You can 'model' the sort of leadership behaviour you'd like to see, and others may start to copy it. Secondly, whether leading or part of the team, you now have a stake in an organizational unit which is larger than you alone. That unit will have more impact on the organization than you would on your own.

'Headroom'

In his book *Making It Happen* (Collins 1988), John Harvey-Jones introduces the concept of *headroom* in the context of empowering individuals to act innovatively in organizations. He writes:

[A] characteristic of a switching-off organization is that there are far too many people and far too many layers so that each employee feels that he has little or no headroom. In such an organization you feel hemmed in by people who can refuse you permission to do something or who are only waiting to jump all over you if you appear to be taking the initiative, or achieving something which even they may recognize as being highly desirable, in 'the wrong way'.

Conversely, when people have lots of 'headroom', they are able to move – mentally as well as physically.

What this means for us, sitting in our cramped bomb turrets watching for opportunities for leverage, is that we should develop 'headroom antennae'. Just as a cat's whiskers let it know when a gap is wide enough for it to pass, so our headroom antennae should let us know when there is some space within which we can act. Here are some of the ways extra headroom happens:

- Changes at the top. The general upheaval will create temporary headroom for everyone – act quickly, though, because things will soon be pegged down again.
- Organizational attention shifts away from your 'patch'. There's nothing so cramping as having the organizational spotlight on your particular area of operations – suddenly everyone wants to meddle in sales, or finance, or quality. Wait till the spotlight swings away to the next flavour of the month; then you can get some real creative work done.
- Your boss changes. Some of the repetitive and destructive patterns you have got into with your old boss will disappear and before new ones take their place you have – headroom!
- The pace of work slackens. This usually happens during holiday periods or when a large project has been completed. Don't tread water; now's your chance to use the headroom this temporary break in activity gives you.
- You achieve a significant and acknowledged success. This will bring in its train a period of time in which your headroom increases.

Autonomy

Even in the most style-cramping organizations, there are places, activities, times when you are less cramped than others. You need to identify those places, activities and times because they are where you're most likely to have sufficient headroom to create. And just as you can widen a crack little by little by wiggling a pen at its weakest point, so you can work your creativity outwards from these points of maximum autonomy.

For example, one individual – I shall call him Dave – had his boss breathing down his neck on apparently every issue. After a bit of thought, Dave realized the only place he had any real autonomy was in his working relationship with his secretary. So he decided to manage his secretary in the way he wished his boss would manage him: delegating as much as possible, consulting over how they would work best together, giving his secretary every opportunity to use her initiative and skills. One consequence of this was that Dave's boss's secretary started to try and change the way his boss worked with *her*, because she also preferred a much more trusting, delegating approach. It's not certain yet whether the boss's style will fundamentally change in the desired direction, but Dave has had the satisfaction of bringing about some change in the managerial style in his organization.

Here are some other questions to help you identify those points that may be opportunities for you to initiate change:

- What kinds of decisions I make are least likely to be challenged by my superiors?
- What projects do I feel I have most determined the direction of?
- What area of my activities is my boss most ignorant of? (Often, your boss knows relatively little about your area of technical expertise, for example.)
- Where can I complete the task successfully alone without reference to anyone else?
- When do I feel most competent?
- When do I feel most self-sufficient?
- When do people most look to me for direction and counsel?

Successful leverage: a case study

Here is the story of one person who identified the leverage points for change and used them so successfully that she now works in a way totally different from most of her peers, a way that is generally acknowledged to be more effective, and a way which she determined herself.

Laura is an educational psychologist. She works for a local education authority – a highly bureaucratic, conservative type of organization. She has, like most educational psychologists, a punitively heavy case load, which should mean that she, like her colleagues, is permanently overworked, at the mercy of a six-month waiting list of children to see her and with no time to do anything but the most cursory diagnostic and advisory work on each child. Not only that, but she has a boss who is totally unsupportive, and an office environment in which she has to discuss work with senior colleagues who will do anything to make the next step on the promotion ladder.

Within this organization and this environment, Laura operates with a commitment that no child will have to wait longer than two weeks to see her, that she will spend significant amounts of her time working with teachers – training them, counselling them, co-working with the most difficult children – that she will engage in counselling work with any child referred to her and his or her family. So she may see a family once a week for six weeks, or once a month for a year. In short, she has created for herself a totally different working pattern from that of the standard educational psychologist, one which she finds more rewarding, which her clients say is more effective, and which she is now helping her colleagues to develop. And she achieved all this from the 'bottom' of the organization. How did she do it?

First, she identified where she could have autonomy. In her professional practice with children, families and teachers, she made the decisions about how to intervene productively, and the educational bureaucracy – providing she acted with professionalism and tact – did not interfere. So at the beginning of her career she focused on developing her expertise, she invested in that, she worked at it until, within her area of most autonomy, she was exceptionally skilled. She had, if you like, created her powerbase.

She then used that power-base to remove a huge block to her creativity: absence of time. She negotiated a lower than average case load in exchange for a commitment to help colleagues and teachers develop some of the skills she had developed. In fact, she could do this by getting them to work *with* her on cases, using a technique of co-working and supervision she had learned through her study in family therapy. So in fact time was released by this approach for her to work more intensively and more effectively with each child (synergy).

As her reputation for excellent practice spread, she used it to build relationships not just with her boss but with her boss's boss (spotting leverage points, again). She began to be asked for her opinion on broad policy matters in education.

Her investment in her colleagues – helping them develop their skills and find a more rewarding way to do their job – meant they listened to her and were committed to her way of working (leverage again). It guaranteed that they would continue to support her workstyle in the future, and it made it likely that they would seek to adopt it as a standard.

And so this single, not very hierarchically elevated, individual became an effective change agent in one of the most bureaucratic organizations there is.

4

Love Me, Love My Change: Influencing Skills

Influence is better than power

'Influence' is defined in *Chambers English Dictionary* as 'the power of producing an effect, [especially] unobtrusively'. This straightforward definition captures the essence of influencing, and it is immediately clear why influencing skills need to be in the toolkit of an aspiring change agent.

In fact, influencing skills are even more important than may at first appear. Those of us who are not at the top of organizations or institutions often cherish the illusion that those who are have power, and that it is only because we don't have power that we have to develop influencing skills.

But the reality is that very few people have true power nowadays. If we define power as the right and capability to make happen what you want to happen, then who has it? Who ever had it apart from absolute monarchs, dictators or tyrants? There are still some organizations where there is a single or family owner wielding considerable power; but you can bet that most people who supposedly occupy that straight and narrow platform 'at the top' think more about responsibility than they ever do about power.

There are also some good reasons for not choosing outright power, even if it is offered you. Of course, we all know that 'power corrupts'. This is meant in the moral sense, but power corrupts in other ways, too. Too much power makes you dull, eating away at your creativity and nimbleness – because you don't need to think carefully to justify your actions, you lose the capacity to think carefully.

In addition, all the evidence suggests that in most cases the more power you have the more temporary that power is likely to be. You are exposed; the temptation to take a pot shot at you, both literally and metaphorically, is great; that is, of course, why tyrants are surrounded by strong military elites. Power distances you and often alienates you from your fellow human beings. How can you be sure they are telling you the truth, since they are probably frightened of you? How can you be sure they are choosing your company for your own sake and not in order to be close to the seat of power?

These reasons no doubt underlie many people's choice to be influential (the president's right-hand man) rather than powerful (the president himself). Of course, there isn't much room at the top, and many people recognize that since they'll never get there, at least to influence the top is better than nothing.

But the kind of influencing I want to talk about in this chapter shouldn't be seen as second best. It is in fact better than power, for three reasons: first, it requires and challenges you to develop your creativity, your quick-wittedness, your capability; second, it will lead to a permanent ability to change the course of events in a direction of your choosing; and third, it will enable you to get and stay close to many different kinds of people.

So the first important principle of influencing emerges:

> To influence is often better than to wield power

Influence in a 'change environment'

Influencing skills are even more important in a 'change environment' than in a stable one. If you invest a lot of time and effort *positioning* yourself in the organization and derive your ability to affect the course of events from your position, then when the pack is shuffled and the position is lost, you are back to square one. If instead you build lots of relationships with people throughout the organization, and come to be seen as someone who is worth listening to, then when the pack is shuffled you have new lines of influence.

Also, while you can set the direction of a change by diktat, you can usually only make that change stick by influence. You can't

44

order people to commit to your change (well you can, but then all you get is lip-service); but you can influence them to see your change as worth investing in.

All the above establishes not only the importance of influencing skills but their rewarding nature. In fact, in organizational life there are few things as personally satisfying as a successful piece of influencing.

Drawing the line at manipulation

Before we look at some more of the basic principles of influencing, we must just draw a clear distinction between *influencing* and *manipulating*.

To manipulate is to bring about an effect, surreptitiously, for one's own personal gain. The primary objective is self-seeking. Hence a manipulator is seen as a 'user' – he or she will use the time and goodwill of others to serve his or her own selfish purposes.

But an influencer, in contrast, can be seen as a giver. True, many manipulators are expert at influencing, but many influencers are in no sense manipulative. Their primary objective is not self-seeking. An influencer is someone who wants to bring about a change, and uses his or her networks and skills to bring it about. Often the change will be to do with making the organization more effective, more productive, more alive, or more interesting. True, this is likely to have a positive impact on the influencer's own working life, but that is not the primary objective.

I think many people shy away from developing influencing skills, because they think that possessing such skills will make them manipulative. That is not so: it is a self-seeking attitude which makes people manipulative; influencing skills simply make them effective.

Some basic principles of influencing

There are some fundamentals to influencing: we have already

come across one, which is that influencing should not be seen as second best, but as something worth practising in its own right.

We'll take a look at some of the other fundamentals before going on to consider in more detail how you can develop as an influencer.

Leverage points

We've used this concept already in Chapter 3. In influencing it's vital to be able to judge when and where to apply the pressure. Good influencers are always on the look-out for leverage points.

Timing

This is really a sub-category of 'leverage points', but it's so important it deserves special mention. In influencing, timing is all. You can say the same thing at two different times, and it will be ignored at one time and acted upon at another. Poor influencers are often ineffective, not because of *what* they say, but because of *when* they say it. They are too early or too late.

One individual I've worked closely with is of the 'lay my cards on the table' persuasion. He always states his position or view too early, before he has given himself the chance to hear where his colleagues are coming from. His often sound views are rarely influential, because people feel they were formed without taking their own into account – they must have been, mustn't they, since he expressed them so early on in the discussion? No matter if he had correctly anticipated their views without having to hear them (which he often does); the people whom he is trying to influence experience him as seeing only his own point of view.

Speaking too early is more common then speaking too late, and I suspect it happens because people feel if they don't get their point in early, they won't get it in at all. It is therefore read, quite rightly, as a sign of weakness and renders the individual even less influential.

In fact, you can picture the course of organizational decision-taking rather like a wave (see figure 3). The greatest leverage point in terms of timing is often when the decision is about to be made: a light touch on the tiller here will have large effects on the direction of the decision.

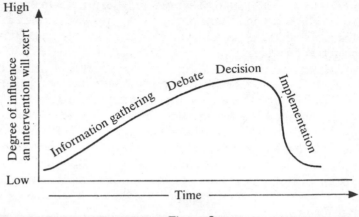

Figure 3

A few people leave their interventions till too late – and are perceived as irrelevant, out of touch, however good their arguments are. In fact, they may be treated with scorn – 'it's easy to be wise after the event' – since there's nothing people dislike so much as a smart alec telling them that the decision they have just worked so hard to make is wrong.

Good influencers develop a fine sense of timing

To be seen *as influential is to* be *influential*

The ability to exert influence is often a self-fulfilling prophecy, in that individuals who are perceived to be influential are often asked for their opinions and have increased opportunity to exert influence. Conversely, who listens to someone who is perceived as uninfluential? The reasoning goes: 'If what she said were worthwhile, people would be acting on it'. This is by no means always true, but most people behave as if it were.

The importance of being seen as having influence means that it is enormously better to make few, but effective, interventions than to make twice as many, only half of which are effective. In

47

other words, it is often the ratio of effective to ineffective interventions which is most important, particularly in the early stages of building influence – you need to make sure that ratio is as high as possible.

You achieve this by making good judgements about which issues your view is most likely to carry weight on, and confining your attempts to influence to those issues until you have stacked up a fair number of 'successes'. Before you intervene ask yourself, 'Do I have special knowledge here?' 'Do I have the most up-to-date information which others don't have?' 'Do I have a record of achievement in this area?' 'Do I have some credibility with this group of people?' Unless the answer to at least one of these questions is 'Yes', don't risk an attempt at influencing.

I had the interesting opportunity to observe a colleague in a series of meetings once (I was understudying for his role at the time). After one of these meetings, at which my colleague had said very little and what he had said seemed to me pretty straightforward, one of the clients present took me to one side and said of my colleague: 'David doesn't say much, but what he does say is always spot on.' I then observed with interest the extent to which David's comments influenced the decisions taken at those meetings, simply by virtue of their rarity!

In fact, David confided to me subsequently that he felt shy in meetings and for a long time didn't think he had much useful to contribute. This was the real reason behind his 'strong and silent man of few words' approach.

Good influencers make sure they are seen to have
a high *proportion* of successes

Feedback

People in positions of power issue edicts, and then walk away, like the Queen crying 'Off with her head' in *Alice in Wonderland*. (Only, unlike the Red Queen, they walk away knowing their edicts will be carried out.)

People who want to exert influence, however, must check out how people feel about their decisions. They must seek feedback at all times. The very act of seeking and receiving feedback increases your influence (since so few people do it) as well as giving you vital information in planning your next bit of influencing. It also reinforces the view of you as confident and influential enough to be open to feedback. Weak people hit and run; strong people hit and wait.

Good influencers are always open to feedback

Types of influencing

How do you know if you are already a good influencer? Reading the principles above should have helped you somewhat, since if you're a good influencer you probably will have recognized your own behaviour in some of them.

But you can also ask yourself these questions:

- Do people listen to me in meetings?
- Do people seek my views on important things?
- Do people tell me about things which matter to them?
- Do I feel as if I count?

And you can always put your influencing skills to the acid test: decide on a change objective, a new state of affairs you want to bring about. Decide whom to influence and when. Implement your plan. Did it work?

The reality is, of course, that we could all do with improving our influencing skills. For even people who are good influencers make bad mistakes sometimes, often because they get tired (and lose subtlety), care *too* much about the outcome (you have to have a little detachment to influence effectively), or get over-confident (and start acting as if they have power).

So let's think about some different types of influencing, to help those of us who aren't good at it yet to get started and those of us who are to extend our range.

Who you know

This type of influencing is based on networking, on cultivating useful relationships with lots of people. After all, if no one knows who you are, it's difficult for you to influence people; and indeed, while some influencers major in this type of influencing, it must to some extent be part of every influencer's toolkit.

How do you network? Some people appear 'naturals' at this; we can learn a lot by watching how they behave:

- They are usually good listeners. They are interested in other people. They ask others about themselves.
- They keep accurate maps of interpersonal relationships. You can see them working out: where does she fit? Whom else does she know? Where does she sit in the company? Whose boss is she?
- Behind most good networkers is a system for remembering whom they've met, when, and where. I know several networkers who keep a running record for all their key contacts of when they spoke last. It's an effective reminder of when to speak again.
- They engage in lots of activities which encourage getting to know people: golf, eating out, yachting, church, social clubs.
- They always respond positively to a phone call, an invitation, someone starting up a conversation. If you want to network, you cannot risk turning people down: remember, even mild rejection hurts and you may not get a second chance.
- They are not cliquy. They will strike up a conversation with anyone. They are considered to be even-handed with their time and affections.
- They are very unlikely to forget a person or a commitment. They are characterized by still having links with, taking an interest in, people from way back in their past.
- People come first for them. They don't mind being interrupted.

- They are usually outstandingly courteous and well-mannered socially.
- They don't name-drop; they don't make the person they're with at the moment feel small by referring to an infinitely more important third party.

These are some of the ways in which networking influencers establish and maintain their influence.

What you know

If you are by nature not a very sociable person and the thought of networking makes you shudder, that does not mean you cannot become influential. You might prefer to do it by *what* you know, rather than *who* you know.

If you think back to the story of Laura in Chapter 3, you will see that one of the ways in which she exerted influence was by winning her colleagues' and superiors' respect for her professional skills, that is, for what she knew. This is a worthy and substantial route to influence, where the influence you exert will not be based on hype or on creating false impressions of importance, but on real knowledge and skill which you have and which others want to benefit from.

Mind you, if knowing a lot were a failsafe route to exerting influence, there would not be so many very knowledgeable, skilful individuals in organizations being told what to do by ignorant self-promoters; nor would so many technical experts be unemployed.

People who know a lot but who exert little or no influence have probably made one or more of the following mistakes:

- They assume that knowing a lot is the only thing that matters. This makes them arrogant, or parochial, or self-absorbed. They think that knowledge itself will advance the cause, that if enough facts are amassed to prove that a certain course of action or change is right, then people will see it and act accordingly.

  In fact, most organizations take a very jaundiced view of

apparent facts. After all, many of the facts they might like to know – because they are of genuine significance to their operations, such as facts about the economy, the markets, the competition – are so tentative, so liable to fluctuation or misinterpretation, because of the complex data on which they are based.

- They develop a narrow portfolio of skill to a very high level. Then they are supremely vulnerable to organizational change. So the whiz-kid programmers are out of a job once the company has the systems it needs and only seeks to maintain them. The specialist aerodynamicists are in deep trouble when the company cuts back on its research and development budget. Narrow technical experts can plummet from being the most valued and influential group to the most vulnerable disfranchised group faster than any other part of an organization.

- They think others will make the effort to communicate with them; they assume others will be interested and will work hard to get involved. They allow themselves to use their specialist jargon in general meetings; they may even think it impresses. In fact, for all of us, skill and technical experts as well as administrators, managers and generalists, the onus is on us to communicate if we want to be heard.

- They permit themselves the luxury of holding less specialist, less skill-based, less knowledge-based functions in contempt. They discount the generalists, the marketeers, the organizational politicians. They allow themselves to believe: 'Anyone can do that. What's really difficult is to master a specialist area, as we have.' Not only does this guarantee that the specialists will become more and more isolated, less and less influential, it is also the basis for profound cracks which will lead to a changing organization ultimately splitting open and falling apart. You can see this happening in the relationship between academics and administrators in many of our universities; and in that between the medical people and administrators in many of our hospitals.

How you talk

The usefulness and the limitations of what you *know* lead naturally on to a third type of influencing, based on how you *communicate*. For in influencing, communication is all.

We have a very ambivalent attitude to persuasive talkers. On the one hand, we envy them their success at bringing about the outcome they want; on the other hand, we imply that *all* they can do is talk. 'He's got the gift of the gab' isn't really a compliment; it suggests a certain vacuousness, lack of substance, behind the words. We are suspicious of the 'smooth talker', and in many traditional organizations a certain roughness of speech, a strong dialect, even a tendency to trip up over words, is likely to endear a leader to his or her followers – even though a 'smooth talker' might be better able to argue the whole organization's interests in the corridors of power.

This ambivalent attitude makes many people highly suspicious of learning to use their communication style better to 'win friends and influence people'. There's a sort of ju-juistic fear that by doing this we will compromise our integrity, become a smooth-talking 'salesman' with no substance.

Other civilizations, other cultures, have had very different attitudes to developing powerful communication skills. In ancient Greece oratory was a vital part of a nobleman's education; Americans are taught it at school – and in work I do with mixed groups of American and British managers the difference in ability to present and argue a case convincingly is staggering. American managers often leave their British counterparts looking tongue-tied and stumped, although they undoubtedly know just as much.

So if we want to exert influence, we have to shake off our snobbish prejudice against the fine art of smooth talking and develop some of the following skills.

Put yourself in your listener's shoes

Raise first the points which matter most to her. Use the illustrations which will carry most weight with her. Speak the language she speaks.

Make your voice interesting to listen to

It's perhaps surprising how often it is the quality of the voice – and not the content – which determines who is listened to. You need to speak with as much variety in tone, emphasis and pace as you can (while still sounding natural!), and to smile when you're speaking if it's at all appropriate. Use your voice as an instrument. Remember, it is difficult for people to listen, and while we all tend to find the sound of our own voice riveting, that experience is unlikely to be shared by our audience.

Use the tone and cadence of your voice to add emphasis to the parts of what you say that you really want people to attend to. I have heard complete banalities uttered as if they were the key to the meaning of life; and because that's the way they were uttered, that's the way they were received.

Study 'smooth talkers', people who can sway meetings, people who get listened to. You need to work out your own style, but you can pick up lots of useful tips from others.

Use humour

People like to laugh. If you can make them laugh, you'll get far more 'air-time'; people will perk up when it's your turn to speak. But take care not to indulge too much in humour at other people's expense; that kind of humour has a tendency to turn round and bite you when you least expect it. People like to laugh; they hate to be laughed at. The experts in the put-down tend to have short-lived influence.

Develop a sense of air-time

Just as you would have to pay dear for a slot on the radio or television, so you can only afford to take up a limited amount of air-time in most organizational contexts. Bosses are busy; meetings are full of people who want to speak; everyone feels they get talked at more than they get heard.

If you are at a meeting with ten other people, every two minutes you speak for potentially lengthens the meeting by 20 minutes. So use your air-time well, and use it at the right times. If the first thing you say is succinct and to the point, you're more likely to get a second hearing. Everything you say should 'add value' in terms of progressing the discussion; bite your tongue and resist the temptation to waste air-time scoring points.

Use your eyes

Look at the people you are talking to, all of them. Involve them with your eyes.

Ask questions

The insightful probing question has turned the course of more decisions than the authoritative statement ever did. Barristers know the power of the targeted question; aspiring influencers need to learn it.

Questions are particularly useful when you want to replace someone else's suggestion with one of your own. Rather than state your alternative suggestion baldly, in clear opposition, explore the original plan with relentless interest. 'How exactly would that solve the problem?' 'How much would it cost – both now and in maintenance long term?' 'Who would need to be involved?' The key here is to explore the weaknesses of the plan, whilst appearing merely to be examining its implications neutrally.

Paint word pictures

If you can capture people's imaginations, you are two-thirds of the way there. Painting word-pictures is a way to do this, because it takes things out of the totally abstract – where you can easily lose people's attention – into something concrete which will set them thinking. A colleague of mine, much listened to by all kinds of people, draws on ordinary everyday experiences for her pictures even when discussing the most elevated organizational issues. I have heard her talk to a managing director about his management style by referring to a swimming pool, describe sophisticated assessment techniques by drawing analogies with colour photography, and get senior managers to understand the importance of good accounting practice by referring to the family budget. A senior manager in the production function of a large manufacturing organization once ruefully said to me that he had a picture of the people who report to him arranging their functions like a fruit and vegetable stall, neat and piled high; he would come along periodically and, literally, upset the applecart, meaning to introduce some development and flexibility into their rigid systems; they would then spend the entire time up to his next visit replacing all the fruit and vegetables exactly as they had been before. As an image of futile activity this takes some beating. The more you can make pictures come alive inside your listeners' heads, the more they will listen to you and you can influence them.

Practise

You might like to listen to a tape-recording of yourself talking – it can be a horrifying but very illuminating experience! Good talking is an art: it repays thought and practice many, many times over.

Research, analysis and detail

All the above three types of influencing are focused on you, the influencer, developing your capability. We cannot leave this central topic without looking at the fourth basis for influencing, which should play some part in every piece of influencing you set out to do.

The more you know about the people you're trying to influence, the context in which you're trying to influence, the history of the issue, the hidden agendas, the stakes people have in particular outcomes, the more effective you'll be as an influencer.

Here are some of the questions you should find answers to:

- Who will make the decision? What's her perspective?
- Who else is trying to influence? How and why? Can I make them into allies?
- What are the rules of the game here? What arguments are legitimate, what illegitimate?
- What's the acceptable currency of the arguments? Is it money, loss of face, people, morality, something else?

- What's the timescale?
- What's gone on before?
- What's in it for all of the key players?
- What are the biggest fears of the key players? What's the best that could happen?

Of course, one is often trying to influence 'by the seat of one's pants'. And skilful influencers pick up clues to the answers to these questions as they go. But wherever you have the opportunity to engage in the kind of research, analysis and detail I've described above, don't hesitate to do so. Salesmen call it 'knowing your target', and it's an invaluable tool.

If 'knowing your target' sounds too Machiavellian for your taste, think of it as showing an interest in the issue you want to affect. After all, why should you be allowed to breeze in and throw your influencing weight around without doing people the courtesy of understanding, literally, where they're coming from?

5

One Man's Chosen Change is Another Man's Imposed Change: How to Deal with Resistance to Change

To describe someone's naturally cautious reactions when the status quo is threatened as 'resistance to change' is already to take up a somewhat unhelpful position. For 'resistance to change' conjures up images of a donkey digging in its heels, a negative action, an objector; it might be better to talk in terms of 'guarding stability'.

Resistance to change is not always a bad thing, and that has to be well understood if one is to overcome it. It can spring from a genuine desire not to see good practice thrown away, or from a concern that the change has been insufficiently thought through.

So the first and most important principle when one meets with apparent resistance to change is: listen to it. Let me illustrate with an example.

A record-keeping organization, whose main income derived from the service it provided to financial institutions, had been failing to make a profit for years. This had not mattered originally, because it was a subsidiary of a much larger company, which had taken the view that the record-keeping activities provided useful entries into potential clients for its other more profitable services. The structure of the record-keeping organization was that a middle manager would have a portfolio of clients; he (for they were all men) would keep in direct personal contact with these clients and they would relate to the organization through him. He had considerable autonomy in negotiating prices and tailoring the service to meet individual needs.

New management at the top of the overall company put in

place a new strategy which dictated that the record-keeping organization must become profitable in its own right. It laid down a different pricing policy: rather than continue to provide an economical 'bargain basement' service, the organization should invest in information technology in order significantly to upgrade its service and start charging premium prices for it.

As is often the case, the people in direct contact with the clients were not involved in determining this new strategy. Nevertheless, they were expected to implement it, and to negotiate increased prices with their customers by 'selling' the improved-quality service.

They knew most about customers' reaction to the change. And what they knew could have been invaluable in helping the organization implement the strategy in the most effective way possible, in setting the timescales, in setting the targets.

The customers were, like most customers, suspicious of the change. They saw – correctly – that it was something the organization was doing first and foremost for itself, not for them. In addition, they made some quite specific points about what kind of service they might be prepared to pay more for, and about which improvements were in fact of little or no interest to them.

You might think that the middle managers were asked to collect all their information and feed it into the decision-making process. You would be wrong.

Early on in the whole development, the middle managers had demonstrated themselves to be resistant to the change. They felt it was an implicit criticism of the way they had done things up to that point; they didn't like having to negotiate higher prices; they were worried that ultimately the new-technology systems would put them out of a job. They had dispatched critical memos to senior management; they had been difficult and obstreperous at briefings; they had been dilatory in negotiating new rates.

Senior management had perceived this resistance, and so had decided to cut these middle managers even further out of the decision-making process. All their reports of customer dissatisfaction were discounted as simply more evidence of *their* resistance to change. As a consequence the organization lost out on a great deal of information which would have helped it implement its strategy more effectively.

There are two lessons to learn from this story. First, don't allow yourself to be labelled as 'resistant to change' if you want to have real influence over that change. Second, don't assume that just because someone is resistant to change he has nothing useful to say on the subject. The more you understand resistance to change, where it comes from and what its nature is, the better able you will be to overcome it both in yourself and in others.

If you refer back to Chapter 1 you will find there much that is relevant on how and why individuals' reactions to change differ, and you will remember that resistance to change often derives from lack of self-esteem, lack of flexibility, or lack of curiosity. But before we look a little further into why in an organizational context these factors can be very significant and how best to approach them, we should take a look at the course of events, feelings, reactions that we typically go through when a change is suggested to us.

Stage 1 is *detached interest*. The length of this stage will vary according to how threatened we personally feel by the change; if we feel *very* threatened this stage may be non-existent. But in many situations, when the possibility of change is first mooted, we may react to it on an intellectual level: 'Oh, that's an interesting idea; I wonder what it would be like exactly.' There is no engagement in or commitment to the change at all at this point; we can take it or leave it, we feel quite separate from it.

Stage 2 is *engaged anxiety*. Once it comes home to us that the change is really on the cards and that it will impact on us, we begin to engage, to take it seriously. And our first emotion is likely to be that of anxiety, fear of loss. Although people in this stage of resistance to change are often difficult to deal with – they argue, they become stressed, they may actively try to sabotage the change – they are in fact much closer to committing to the change than people in stage 1.

Stage 3 is *engaged interest*. At this point resistance to change has gone, and people are actively promoting the change. This is the desired end state for people on whom change is being imposed.

When you are trying to get a change accepted, the way you handle stage 2 is particularly important. If you handle it by downplaying the impact of change, by saying, for example, 'You won't really notice any difference' or 'It won't affect you', then people are likely to go *back* to stage 1 rather than forward to stage 3. You need to offer reassurance *not* that nothing will really change, *but* that people will have the resources and support they need to embrace and cope with the change. You need to make yourself available to answer lots and lots of 'What if?' questions. You need to respond to people's concerns by thinking with them of solutions to possible problems they have raised. It is much better if you respond genuinely to an issue you had not thought of but they had, than if you appear to have 'prepared answers' to everything. The most important thing you need to give people in Stage 2 is *time*, and there are very few organizations that give enough of this in periods of change. The people affected need to talk, question, go away, reflect, come back and question some more.

Getting through stage 2 takes as long as it takes. It's worth spending a lot of time dealing with people's anxiety and not moving on implementation until as many as possible are in stage 3: you'll save time in the long run. Also, some of the people who are most anxious in stage 2 will be most able and willing to promote the change in stage 3. They will have been most anxious because they were really thinking hard about what it would all mean for them, but when they have worked through all of that they will understand the change and all its ramifications.

Again, the message is: listen to and value resistance to change. Only the mindless would allow themselves to be pushed in a different direction without protest.

We have concentrated so far on what I would call 'positive' resistance to change – resistance to change for good reasons, to do with checking out its value, ensuring one's own safety or survival through it, and acquiring some opportunity to influence its course. We need now to consider negative resistance to change, which springs from negative roots and which tends to be destructive even of positive change. As before, we can consider three causes of negative resistance to change.

First, it can result from low self-esteem. Many organizations seem to set about lowering their employees' self-esteem in a systematic, even determined, way; yet I'm sure none would consciously have that as an objective. Reduced self-esteem is an unfortunate spin-off for most of us of being told what to do (implying we could not or would not work it out for ourselves), being criticized more than praised (implying we fail more than we succeed), and being kept in the dark about much that is important or relevant to us in the organization (implying we cannot be trusted).

If all of this does have the expected effect on our self-esteem, then we are likely to cling on to the status quo for dear life, terrified that we won't be able to cope with change or that the organization will use it as an opportunity to ditch us.

Second, it can result from low flexibility. Organizations often, wittingly or unwittingly, end up reducing our flexibility. They turn us into narrow specialists to maximize the short-term return on our skills; they value law-abiding conformism more than rule-breaking exploration; they prefer us to be 'company men' who can be relied on to stay rather than marketable free agents.

It is small wonder that many people experience anger, even bitterness, when the very organization which has coaxed, nurtured and cajoled them into a particular rut decides to change so that ruts like that no longer exist.

And it is hardly surprising that people who have essentially been on an intensive training programme in inflexibility for years should resist change with all their might.

Third, it can result from low curiosity – the 'I've seen it all before' syndrome. Low curiosity often springs from disappointment. It's a way of protecting yourself against being made a fool of. So in organizations where there have been several new initiatives which failed, curiosity about change is likely to hit an all-time low.

The effect of all these kinds of resistance to change is to

prolong stages 1 and 2, detached interest and engaged anxiety, and often to make it wellnigh impossible to move people into stage 3. Ultimately, the organizational roots of negative resistance to change must be tackled if the organization is going to stay healthy and capable of change.

But if you want to bring about a change and haven't the time or the influence to tackle these organizational roots, then the key is not to impose change but to elicit it. It's imposed change that makes people who've been badly treated by the organization dig their heels in; change which they initiate can actually undo some of the damage the organization has done.

For this reason it's often better if you, as a change agent, don't have too fixed an idea about the change you want to bring about. Let's illustrate this point with an example.

Sarah is a technical author in the relevant part of a large software house. She is responsible, together with four other technical authors, for user manuals. Different projects 'buy in' time from the technical author team, and Sarah and her four colleagues spend most of their working hours seconded to these different projects, working with the software writers to understand the programs and write manuals to guide the prospective users of the programs.

Sarah had thought from the beginning of her time with the company that she and her colleagues always seemed to be reinventing the wheel. She would produce a section on database maintenance for one project, and subsequently realize a similar section had been written for another project only a few months ago. Also, she was disturbed that the user manuals she and her colleagues produced had no recognizable 'house style'. They each wrote in their own style. She felt an opportunity to enhance the perceived professionalism of the company was being missed.

Sarah had to tread carefully. She was the 'new girl' in the technical author team. She didn't want to appear critical of how things were, nor did she want to be seen as trying to improve the service they were offering, but she also had an open mind.

She decided to raise the whole question in a fairly low-key way at their next team meeting. She put an item on the agenda: 'Ways to stop repetition and enhance our efficiency'. At the meeting, she raised some of the problems she had faced, and asked her colleagues if they had any suggestions.

They had plenty. The meeting ended up deciding that there should be a catalogued reference system of all manuals produced, with all manual sections sub-classified and cross-referenced; that it should be standard practice to consult the reference system for any relevant material before embarking on a new project (secretaries should be able to do this if the 'library' were set up properly); that they would spend some time working out a house style; and that they would let the rest of the organization know about the changes.

Imagine what might have happened if Sarah had gone into that meeting with a set of proposals rather than a problem she needed help with. The way she handled it meant her colleagues were driving the change, owned it, were committed to it. If she'd tried to push them, they might well have ended up defensive, offended, and driving themselves into a corner where they had to maintain that current practice was best.

One last word, just to make the point. Imagine your boss comes into your office and says: 'We're going open plan. Get ready to lose your office walls.' Now imagine an alternative scenario where he says: 'What do you think we should do about our office overcrowding problem?' In which scenario are you more likely to co-operate with a change?

So much for dealing with other people's resistance to change which you think is a good idea. What about dealing with your own resistance to change? What do you do when you feel that leaden weight in the pit of your stomach, that anxious knot; when all you want to do is hold on tight to what you've got?

- Try to understand where your resistance comes from. Reread this chapter, and Chapter 1.
- Is this reaction typical of you or untypical? Then you'll know if it's a general problem or specific to this particular change. Try asking someone you trust if he or she thinks you're generally frightened of change.

- Is it perhaps the person who's initiating the change that you don't trust, rather than the change itself?
- Face your fear. What are the potential bad consequences for you?
- Write down your reasons for objecting to the change. Leave them for a day or two; then read them – are they reasonable?
- What would have to be said or done to make you feel comfortable with the change, to reassure you? Specify this as precisely as you can.
- Talk to other people whom this change will affect or who have experienced similar changes in the past. Replace your fantasy fears with reality knowledge.
- Are there any good things which might ensue from the change? Think about them.
- Reflect on past change you've survived, maybe even benefited from. Can you draw any parallels?

Sometimes when I feel terrified by change, tempted to spend all my energy in futile resistance to it, I lift myself mentally and emotionally out of the situation, become a spectator of my own life. Then, sometimes not always, I can enjoy the richness and variety of it all. Change is a sign that we are still alive; change is the chance to become more alive still.

You have the right to resist; you also have the opportunity to enjoy.

6

Oil and Grit:
Making Change Happen in Groups

Most tasks which organizations set themselves are too big to be accomplished by a single individual. So, much of organizational life is spent in what we choose to call 'teams': project teams, management teams, functional teams, and so on.

Now, the word 'team' implies quite a high degree of internal structure. Think of a football team, for example, where every member has his own position, particular game objectives, and territory. Not only that, everyone knows immediately the position of everyone else. It is rare for teams in ordinary working life to have this degree of structure, and in some cases there is no structure at all – the team is simply a collection of peers who will divide the job up between them.

Also, the word 'team' implies clearly identified shared goals. Perhaps here the work team has much in common with the sports team, but still there are work teams who have to identify their goals before they start; and there are many where the goals of one part of the so-called team are very different from those of another.

What I am building up to is this: that it is often more appropriate to view teams in organizations not as teams but simply as *groups*.

What's in a name, you may say. In this case, a great deal. The structure and single-mindedness of a true team allow it to sidestep many of the interpersonal problems most commonly referred to collectively as 'group dynamics'; while a loosely structured bunch of people, with varying degrees of commitment to and clarity about what they are to achieve, hits group dynamics head-on and is highly likely to grind to a halt in consequence.

So in this chapter we are going to take a layman's look at group dynamics, the particular problems groups face when approaching change, and how the change agent can work with groups to overcome these problems and release the group energy on the change task. If you want to change things in organizations, sooner or later you are bound to need to do so in or through a group.

Much of what I shall say about the different types of group is based on Bion's theory of groups. Bion was a French psychoanalyst who developed great skill in getting groups to work constructively together; based on his experiences, he formulated a theory which is stunning in its simplicity and powerful in its ability to describe what goes on.

Bion said that groups will often fall into one of three categories: the *fight/flight* group; the *pairing* group; and the *work* group. Which of the categories a group falls into will determine its ability to produce useful work, the well-being of people in the group, and, of particular interest to us here, its ability to adapt and change appropriately.

In describing these types of group, I have modified Bion's theory somewhat. I want to acknowledge where the original insight comes from, but also to make it clear that my version may not be as elegant or consistent with psychoanalytic theory as his. I have sacrificed elegance and consistency for the sake of producing a theory which we can all use reasonably readily.

A fight/flight group

This is a group which is primarily concerned with protecting itself. It sees the external environment, including people outside the group, as threatening; it responds either by withdrawing (flight) or attacking (fight). It has as its most important goal the protection of its own integrity from outside influence. Teams that have been quietly doing productive work on a task can turn into fight/flight groups at the drop of a hat if threatened with being disbanded or split up; they may also react like this if criticized, or if it looks as though they may be given a task they fear they cannot succeed at. Thus one of the things that can happen when you suggest change to a group is that it becomes a flight/fight group.

What are the characteristics of fight/flight groups? How do they behave?

- They reject information which comes from outside the group. Governments in their last stages, when they are about to be overthrown, are perhaps the classic example of this; also company boards which reject financial analyses which indicate their weakness.
- They are very likely to punish the messenger – it's extremely risky to be the bearer of bad news to such groups!
- They will talk a lot among themselves about how stupid, untrustworthy or ill-informed people outside the group are.
- They are likely to spend a lot of their time together planning how they will ensure their own survival.
- They will run lots of meetings behind closed doors.
- Every so often, they will expel a member from the group, because he or she threatens its unity.
- They will be paranoid. They will interpret quite ordinary events or comments as dangerous or malicious to the group.
- They will often have a very strong, authoritative leader whom no one is allowed to challenge.
- They will deny failure, blaming it on unreasonable others.

I can still vividly recall the time when a group of normally fairly amiable senior executives turned into a fight/flight group against me. They had asked me and a colleague to observe a three-hour meeting they were holding and give them some feedback at the end on how well they were functioning as a team. My first, and cardinal, mistake was that I took this request at face value: I thought they genuinely wanted to make progress as a team, to function better, to change. In fact, what they really wanted was reassurance that they were already brilliant.

During the three-hour meeting, I sat and made notes. I soon saw a pattern which I was sure was hampering their effectiveness. First, the leader – a physically small man, but with enormous suppressed energy, an ability to talk for minutes on end with no break, and a tendency to attack first and think later – was the only person who interrupted during the meeting. Despite the fact that he in any event spoke for three-quarters of the time, the remaining ten executives sharing the other quarter between them, he still interrupted and talked over them many times; they never did this to him or to each other. Second, the meeting was not so much a meeting as a set of dialogues between the leader and each of his team. There was hardly ever any discussion and debate between team members. Third, the only person who ever made a decision was the leader.

At the end of the meeting, I got up to give my feedback. I decided to do it by asking them to analyse their own decision-making processes. They refused to do it. They said there was no process to analyse, they simply moved towards decisions as a unit, in a sort of organic way; they worked so well together, they said, that there was no longer any process or any differentiation between individuals' roles.

I was completely flabbergasted by the mismatch between this view and what I had observed. I decided to abandon subtlety and just give them the feedback straight. I described what I had seen, referring to my notes. I should say that in no way did I blame the leader for the patterns I had seen; I regard those kinds of pattern as the joint responsibility of all parties involved. They looked at me in a rather indulgent, slightly pitying way. Then the leader said he thought I had a problem, in that I read too much into things. That was the end of my feedback – and I have to say the end of my credibility with that group.

Afterwards, one of the executives who had been most humiliated by the leader during the meeting took me to one side. 'Why did you attack John (the group leader) like that, Alison?' he said, sounding genuinely puzzled and a little hurt. 'We're all very fond of him, you know – and he's achieved an enormous amount and doesn't get any recognition for it.'

That in fact was the key to the whole débâcle, and the reason why I had approached the group in totally the wrong way (resulting not only in my discomfort, of minor importance to everyone but me, but in the group's team-working, rather than being progressed and *changed*, solidifying even more into limiting and unhelpful patterns). This was a group that was engaged in a very difficult task in a very critical, uncaring organization. Its members could not possibly handle any more criticism; what they were looking for from me was some of the recognition they felt they were owed. Had I responded to that need of theirs first, we might have had a truly productive feedback session.

It is easy to tip groups into fight/flight, just as it is easy to make individuals anxious, when you are trying to introduce change. And a fight/flight group is a formidable opponent; you don't simply *multiply* the resisting powers of one individual by the number in the group, you increase them exponentially.

The pairing group

Unlike the fight/flight group, which is preoccupied with the external environment, albeit in order to fend off real or imagined threats, the pairing group is totally self-absorbed. The primary goal is to form relationships in the group. This kind of group behaves in the following ways:

- It will spend a lot of time together socially.
- It is likely to tell a lot of in-jokes.
- It will have a 'clubby' atmosphere: people may even dress in a particular recognizable style. Sometimes people in a group like this even look physically similar – this is to do with the tendency of groups like this to select new members on the basis of how much they resemble the existing ones.
- There may be quite a lot of sexual activity in the group: people dating, sexual jealousy, competitiveness. All is by no means happy within the boundaries of the group.
- The group will conceal its rivalries and tensions from 'outsiders'; it will prefer to present a chummy, happy front.
- A high proportion of the group's discussion will be about itself, its own members; relatively little will be about things external to the group.

- The group will spend time together even when it doesn't have a task to do.
- It will comprise a network of strong alliances, and will resist attempts to subdivide it for any purpose across these alliances.
- Group members will call themselves 'friends' rather than 'colleagues'.
- Group members' family and personal lives will often take second place to the activities of the group; partners 'outside the group' will not tend to be invited to social functions.
- The group will minimize the risk of failure.

Pairing groups can often be extraordinarily complacent. This makes it extremely difficult to get them to change. And since they don't take a lot of notice of the outside world, it's hard to find a channel into them for information which might lead them to change.

The work group

This is a productive group, focused on a task. It is a true team, in many respects. Often it has been through pairing and/or fight/flight incarnations, and has reached a level of maturity as a group which means that it can interact continuously and profitably with the external environment. Some signs that a group is truly a work group are the following:

- The members will be clear about what needs to be done and their part in doing it.
- The output of the group will be high.
- The group will be ready to disband when the task is complete.
- It will be open to people, ideas and information from outside; indeed it will take conscious steps to stay in touch.
- It will review its own performance, and try to improve.
- It will acknowledge failure, and try to work out why it happened.

Work groups are much more open to change that they perceive will progress their task than are fight/flight or pairing groups.

The power of the system

In addition to the particular problems associated with fight/flight and pairing groups, there are some general problems when it comes to groups and change that derive from the central characteristics of a group. A group is a *system* – even when it isn't a team, there is some internal structure, individuals are defined in relation to others in the group, and, if the group is stable, they will behave in a way which is consistent with their place in the group. The group will have achieved equilibrium in the context of the way things are; if they're going to change, the group will have to lose its current equilibrium before it finds a new one. Nobody likes losing his or her balance, and there will be strong 'bolstering forces', trying (not always consciously) to keep the group stable at the expense of change. The change agent has to overcome these.

There are two main ways for the change agent to do this. One is to lower the level of perceived threat so that the group feels safe to change; the other is to raise the level of perceived threat so that the group feels it is too dangerous not to change. I call these two ways 'oil' and 'grit', respectively, because 'oil' reduces friction and makes it easier for mechanical parts to move in relation to each other, whilst the proverbial 'grit in the oyster' produces constructive change – in the form of a shining pearl – by increasing friction and 'aggravating' the system. Both oil and grit 'work' in the sense of bringing about change; the method you choose will depend on your personality and the situation.

Oil

The change agent who chooses to influence groups via 'oil' behaves in the following ways:

- He takes every opportunity to raise the self-esteem of the group and of the individuals within it: he may do this with actual praise and encouragement or simply by listening attentively, giving of his time and interest, demonstrating that the group matters.

- He is patient: he moves at the group's pace; he does not try to rush decisions or actions.
- He acts to reduce tension between group members: he points out to people where they agree, where their arguments support each other; he helps communication by restating, translating. Part of his stock-in-trade is likely to be the phrase 'I think what so-and-so means is . . .', to rephrase something someone has said in a way which is more comprehensible and/or helpful to other people.

The effect of this kind of behaviour is to reduce anxiety, to make people feel it is safe to explore, to criticize, to challenge, to provoke – and ultimately to change. Even one person behaving like this in a group – particularly if that person is perceived to be influential – can have a profound effect on the group's adapting ability. Change is well and truly 'facilitated', that is, made easier, smoother.

'Oil' is particularly appropriate for making progress with fight/flight groups. It would have been a much better approach than the one I took with the group I described earlier.

Grit

The change agent who chooses to influence groups via 'grit' behaves in the following ways:

- She says things which are surprising.
- She challenges the group's assumptions.
- She asks questions which take the group down uncomfortable lines of thought: 'How long do you think things can stay like this?' 'Who is least satisfied with our performance?'
- She refuses to collude, either with the group as a whole or with any individual in it.
- She raises the levels of tension, agrees when people say there's a problem, doesn't reassure, doesn't play down disturbing signs, she escalates.

- She introduces true and relevant but frightening information: 'The profits this year are down to 50% of last year's.' 'Our staff turnover is currently 30% per annum.' 'All departments are having to justify their existence in pure financial terms now.'

All of this she must do in a detached, neutral way. It is her separateness which irks and irritates the group, like the grit in the oyster, maybe producing a pearl of change.

But it may not. It may simply produce anger, hostility and ultimately rejection. And that's where the change agent needs true grit. For it can be very uncomfortable to be the grit in the oyster.

If, behaving in this way, the change agent is seen as having a personal axe to grind, the group can categorize her behaviour, discount her, render her impotent. She must puzzle them, forcing them to look at themselves, not to reject her comfortably as 'the one with the problem'.

Sometimes a prolonged dose of grit is the only thing that will jolt a pairing group out of its complacency. I remember a production unit in a manufacturing organization which had become extremely cosy. The unit's leader was at a loss to get the others to think in terms of becoming sharper, more competitive. They thought they were doing just fine. In the end, he provoked some change by inviting one of the finance team along for the first ten minutes of each of their weekly meetings. The financial man simply presented some figures and then withdrew. The figures were never discussed; the leader would then pass on to item number two on the agenda. But after this had been going on for a few meetings, the group began to discuss ways of improving their efficiency, and actually implemented these. (The figures concerned the relative efficiency of the different production units in the organization.)

I think the real key to the success of this approach was the way those figures were introduced but not discussed. The group must have been thinking 'I wonder what this all means; let's think about it', rather than arguing the figures away and bolstering each other up.

The kinds of skills I have talked about here are among the most advanced tools in the change agent's toolkit. They demand a level of self-control and creativity combined which we aspire to only in our better moments. But even at a more mundane level, it's worth remembering that when we're part of a group there will be even stronger forces trying to maintain the status quo than normal. We need to practise 'helicoptering' out of the group, detaching ourselves from it, and working out how best to help it make progress – whether we lead it, are just one of its members, or are merely invited to participate briefly in its activities.

One more point before we leave the subject of groups and change. To know whether you can act as an *agent provocateur* and move a group forward, you have to ask yourself some searching questions. Not only must you be sure you don't want to influence the group simply to settle an old score, or make yourself feel important, but you must also ask:

- *Do you believe in this group?* If in your heart of hearts you don't believe it can do good work, you're not the right person to be oil or grit for it.
- *Do you like this group?* If you don't, you'll want to break it up; the group will sense it and immobilize you.
- *How important is it to you to belong?* If it's very important, you will be unable to detach yourself sufficiently to be useful to the group as a change agent. You will be looking for short-term approval rather than long-term effectiveness.
- *Are you scared of this group?* If you are, don't embark on changing it. And don't be ashamed of being scared – groups are frightening.

7

Caught not Taught:
How to Develop the Next Generation
of Change Agents

I am sure that if you want other people to welcome and enjoy change, the best thing you can do is to let them see you welcoming and enjoying it. It is in this sense that change agency is caught, not taught. I remember a totally unconvincing conference I went to on 'Managing Change': the chairman was a comfortable-looking chap in his fifties, who, while he said all the right things between speakers, exhorting us all to get excited about change and stay flexible, betrayed his own fundamental focus on stability and predictability by sticking rigidly to the timetable even when there were good opportunities for prolonged and lively debate. I can still picture him, peering at the watch he had carefully placed on the bench in front of him, and hear him sounding more pleased that we had broken for lunch on the dot of 1 o'clock than he had at any of the contributions we had heard during the morning. I can no longer remember anything that was said about change on that day.

So as managers of others and as influential colleagues, we will be watched far more than we will be listened to, in matters of change as in all matters. If we are enthusiastic and flexible, this approach is likely to spread to those around us; if we are fearful and rigid, so is this. If we work hard to turn good ideas into reality, people will learn one thing from us; if we play with new ideas, day in day out, with nothing really 'sticking', they will learn another.

Incidentally, I am convinced that parents and educators can play a key role in bringing about new attitudes to change. If our children see us taking all the changes that abound now in our stride, hear us discussing new ways with enthusiasm, share lives

76

with us that involve changing roles, changing jobs, changing cultures, changing assumptions, then, they will be much better equipped to make the best of the changes they encounter than we or our parents ever were. In her book *My Mother, My Self* (Fontana 1988), Nancy Friday says that instead of saying to our children as they leave for school in the morning 'Take care, dear', we should say 'Take lots of risks today, dear'. It's a nice idea, and fits well with the attitude to change we are talking about in this book.

Still, given that at work we are for the present surrounded by people who like ourselves are often afraid that they have more to lose than to gain from change, what can we do, apart from being obvious change agents ourselves, to help others become change agents? I am talking here of day-to-day managerial style, not of big organizational decisions (some of which we looked at in Chapters 4 and 5).

I have formulated some concrete suggestions in terms of the kind of manager that brings out and nurtures change agency in the people who report to her (let's assume the manager is female throughout this chapter, in the true spirit of change!).

The disclosing manager

Managers who share information as much as they can, who encourage people to ask questions, and who spend time talking about organizational issues rather than simply issuing directives, breed change agents. They are giving people what they need in order both to have new ideas which are relevant and to feel comfortable when their part of the organization changes.

The disclosing manager is the opposite of the 'need to know' manager; she thinks it is always better to tell people things unless there is a strong argument to the contrary. I have spent a lot of my professional life as a consultant to defence-related organizations, and one of the problems such organizations have in trying to promote a change culture derives from the ubiquitousness of the 'need to know'. It becomes easier to keep people in the dark, to keep them narrowly focused on their immediate job, as a first resort, so that not only genuinely confidential information but also all sorts of straightforward organizational facts are concealed. The habit of questioning is discouraged. People are not likely to network. None of this derives from any particular tyrannical or repressive desire on the part of the people at the top of these organizations; it is simply an inappropriate extension of the 'need to know' principle.

Mind you, there are plenty of 'need to know' managers in non-defence-related industries. These are typically managers who lack confidence, and who seek to bolster the importance of their own position by refusing to share information with their subordinates. They would espouse a strictly hierarchical view of information access: the higher up you are, the more you should know. And conversely, the lower down you are, the less you should know.

The disclosing manager, by contrast, believes that information should go to whoever can make good use of it, regardless of hierarchical position. Of course, organizations will always have commercially confidential information which has to be protected, but the disclosing manager recognizes that this must be kept to a minimum if she is to encourage flexibility and initiative in her staff – in short, if she is to develop change agents.

It is only by understanding as broad an organizational perspective as possible that people will begin to see leverage points for change and spot opportunities for innovation and improvement. Also, when they are told more, they become less fearful and less suspicious, and they feel more valued, all attitudes essential to change agency, as we have seen.

By 'the disclosing manager', I do not mean the loose talker who cannot keep her counsel. The disclosing manager uses communication in just as self-disciplined a way as the 'need to know' manager, but she disciplines herself to communicate rather than to refrain. I know disclosing managers who hold informal 'ask-me' sessions every week over coffee or lunch: it requires a lot of organization and discipline to keep this up, especially when the pressure of the job is high. But these are the managers who get the most from their staff, not just in terms of change agency but also in terms of 'ordinary' achievement.

The coaching manager

The coaching manager gets alongside the people who report to her, looks with them at the problems they are trying to solve, allows them to watch her try out solutions, creates opportunities for them to see her succeed *and* fail. In doing this, she encourages the spirit of partnership; it means she can act to increase her people's competence levels without taking away from them their feelings of self-reliance and self-esteem.

The coaching manager spends time finding out how her people succeed and fail, where their strengths and weaknesses are: she focuses on them and not on the task alone. So when they are stuck, or when a job isn't done properly, she doesn't tell them things they know already, making them feel stupid for having been unable to put them into practice; she gives them extra information or teaches them new skills precisely where necessary, reinforcing that they already have plenty of competence and that if they just plug a gap or two their existing competence will be more effective. The coaching manager believes time spent letting people experiment is time well spent.

I have had the good fortune to be managed over the last three years by a coaching manager. She has always identified opportunities as early as possible for me to try new things; but she has always made time to talk through the challenging assignments with me beforehand, to get me to rehearse what I shall do or say if certain things happen, to describe what she would do in the same situation whilst encouraging me to look for different and better ways of handling things. I remember, for example, the first time I presented a paper at a big conference; there was never any question of her doing it instead of me, although at that time she would undoubtedly have done it better. But she made time to listen to me rehearse the presentation, and gave me several tips on how to make it more immediately interesting to that particular audience.

Everything the coaching manager does carries the message: your experience and expertise are already of great value; now we're going to increase their value.

Contrast this with the coaching manager's opposite: the directing manager. When she sees a task being unsuccessfully carried out, she says what's wrong and what has to be done to put it right. She doesn't base this on any understanding of the person involved, simply on the shortfall in the task. She only interacts with her people when she needs to direct their activity. She keeps her own work separate from theirs. She may be sociable and friendly, but when at work she is in charge. She has the answers.

To her, task failure is absolute failure. Tasks are not learning opportunities; they are things to be accomplished. She is always in a hurry.

The visioning manager

A vast amount has been written and even more said about 'leadership' and 'charisma'. The search for the components of charismatic leadership has been a Holy Grail of management studies. It has some relevance to the question of how to manage in order to create change agents. For the essence of change agents is that they pick up the ball and run with it, and they will often run faster than the leader; there is a sense in which they have been energized. And, of course, it is this inspirational quality which people are trying to capture when they talk about charisma.

The key quality of managers who can do this, in our context, is the ability to paint a compelling picture of the future. If you are going to work hard and, indeed, to take risks to reach some future goal, you need to believe in the goal. And to believe in it, you must understand it, see how things will be different when it is reached, have your imagination captured by it.

That is why we can call the manager who can make this happen for her people the 'visioning manager'. She herself is excited by the possibility of change, and can see not only the goal of a specific change but also how the whole picture will be altered and improved. She has the vision. Not only that, but she can also communicate that vision to others.

Many of the large organizations going through major change

build physical models or set up display rooms which employees are encouraged to visit to get a very concrete sense of where the organization is heading. The visioning manager does the same thing for her people, more powerfully, by talking with them about the future.

She doesn't have to be a great orator to do this successfully, although if she is it's certainly useful. But she does need to be able to talk to her people in the words and images they can relate to. And she does need to be able to talk in a way which allows them to see her own enthusiasm.

That is not to say that she has to take the whole responsibility for creating the vision. It's much more important that she enables her people to create their own vision. She will do this by asking, explicitly and implicitly, 'How will things be different round here when. . . ?'

I recently heard a manager who is excellent at doing just this put this question to her people. (The change she was promoting was that managers start setting their people precise objectives.) Here are just some of the answers they came up with:

- There will be less 'sniping' (individuals criticizing each other gratuitously).
- People will be clearer about what they're expected to do.
- People will talk to each other more.
- People will criticize the organization less.
- People will feel less cynical.
- Achievement will matter.
- Profits will rise!

You can appreciate how much more likely these people were to invest in bringing about the change and to implement further associated changes once they had created such a compelling vision for themselves of the pay-offs.

Not only is visioning important when trying to energize people towards specific change, but it is also important for an organization, and therefore for the individuals within it, to develop the *capability* and *will* to vision. Once a majority of people in an organization have come to the view that 'nothing will ever change', that organization is in deep trouble.

The confident manager

Don't confuse confidence with complacency. The complacent manager believes that 'all is for the best in the best of all possible worlds'; the confident manager believes that 'there are some good things and some problems about the way things are, but we'll cope if we put our minds to it'. The complacent manager doesn't acknowledge failure; the confident manager is interested in understanding failure – her own, other people's and the organization's. The complacent manager is *self*-satisfied; the confident manager is satisfied that others, generally, will do OK.

Confident managers are good breeders of change agents for the following reasons:

- They *don't* jump on mistakes and create a risk-averse climate.
- They *do* support their people when they have difficulties.
- They *don't* project anxiety on to others (the classic example of anxiety projection is the manager who rushes out of a pressured meeting with her boss and immediately shortens all the deadlines her people are working to).
- They *do* allow their people to tell them what they are anxious about.
- They *don't* hide problems.
- They *do* act as if most, if not all, problems have solutions.
- They *don't* jump to conclusions.
- They *do* listen.
- They *don't* rush around in a panic.
- They *do* smile.

One of the biggest factors sapping a manager's confidence is the fear that if she brings her people on, they will usurp her and she will become, literally, redundant. So to be truly confident, a manager needs confidence that her value – to this particular organization, to organizations generally – does not depend on other people's incompetence. How can managers be helped to have this kind of confidence?

- by defining the management role sufficiently clearly that she does not see it as merely a 'backstop' or 'safety net' for her subordinates' mistakes;
- by giving her success criteria which are all about increasing other people's value rather than competing with them;
- by encouraging her to investigate, invest in, and increase her own 'marketability' – to this particular organization and more generally (see the next chapter for a fuller discussion of 'marketability').

In many if not most organizations, these conditions do not prevail. So it is likely that we shall all have to cope for much of our careers with managers who are frightened we will usurp them. Understanding this may help us be more detached from their restrictions and criticisms.

Have you got what it takes?

We have seen that managers who breed change agents are those who have a managerial style which is disclosing, coaching, visioning and confident. You probably already have some idea how much of each of these qualities you demonstrate, but to help you work out where you need to make most effort to change your style, here are some questions to answer.

'Managing for change' self-diagnosis quiz

Answer yes or no, as instinctively as you can. If you don't manage people at present, answer in the way you think you *would* behave.

1. Do you tell people about your mistakes?
2. Do you laugh about your mistakes?
3. Are you interested in how people learn?
4. Do people come to you for advice?

5. Are you careful about what you say?
6. Do you often do things yourself because that way they'll be done better?
7. Do you concentrate on today's job, believing tomorrow's will take care of itself?
8. Do you think people are worried by too much information?
9. Do you think managers should take risks to test the limits of people's ability?
10. Do you have any locked drawers or filing cabinets?
11. Do you sometimes get very excited about the project you're working on?
12. Do you often take responsibility for teaching people new skills?
13. Do you try to protect your people from making mistakes?
14. Do you circulate memos as widely as possible?
15. Have you ever been accused of being secretive?
16. Do you often talk to your people about where the organization is heading?
17. Do you like managing people who've just joined the organization?
18. Do you believe 'the buck stops here'?
19. Do you think there's too much loose talk around at work?
20. Do you learn most of what you learn from books and papers rather than people?
21. Do you find it difficult to express your feelings?
22. Do you think you're good at your job?
23. When something's up, do people often come and ask you what you think is going on?
24. Do people often come and ask you for help when they can't do something?
25. Do you worry about your future in the organization?
26. Do you tend to stick to the facts when you are explaining something, rather than embellish or elaborate?
27. Do you enjoy persuading people on subjects which matter to you?
28. Have you ever been indiscreet with a piece of information at work?

29. Do you trust your boss?
30. Are you good at making people laugh?
31. Do you often sit alongside your people when you're talking to them about a task?
32. Do you think a manager should be more competent across the board than the people she manages?
33. Do you quite often find it hard to know what to say?
34. Do you lose your temper often?
35. Do people often chat to you about issues at work?
36. Do you often reassure people when they think they can't succeed?
37. Is it your view that 'the boss knows best' on most issues?
38. Do you enjoy talking to people?
39. Are you good at 'getting to the heart of the matter'?
40. Do you encourage people to 'have a go'?
41. Do you worry a lot that inexperienced people won't produce work of a sufficiently high standard?
42. Are you good at giving presentations?
43. Do you think it is more important as a manager to be discreet than to be open?
44. Do you keep a very close check on how your subordinates are tackling a task?
45. Do you think the person at the top of the organization should be accessible to people at all levels?
46. If you lost this job, do you think you would get another quite easily?
47. Do you often draw or write on a flip chart when you're explaining something?
48. Do you pride yourself on being an excellent delegator?
49. Does your boss come down on you very heavily if you make a mistake?
50. Do you read widely?
51. Do you like to hear your people's views on the key issues for your organization?
52. When people come to you with difficulties over their work, do you spend time discussing with them what they might do?
53. Would people call you an 'enthusiastic' type?

54. Do you hate being criticized?
55. Do your people know what the organization's overall strategy is?
56. Do you try to ensure that you are more competent than your subordinates at most things?
57. Would you say that most of your interest centred on leisure rather than work activities; that you work mainly to earn a living?
58. Do you tell your own boss quite a lot of things about your people and their performance which you don't tell them directly?
59. Do you think many of the people who work for you have the potential to be better than you?
60. Do you think it's important for people to believe in the value of their work?
61. Is work the most important element in your life?
62. Do you spend much more time with your peers than with your subordinates?
63. Do you lose sleep over things that are not going well at work?
64. Do you find much of your work boring?
65. Do you quite often let your subordinates watch you do things?
66. Do you manage each of your subordinates differently, depending on their style?
67. Do you worry that you 'let slip' too much?
68. Do you expect every task to be completed perfectly?
69. Have you ever worked for a truly inspirational boss?
70. Do you feel critical of colleagues who get 'too close' to their subordinates?
71. Are you often frustrated by the incompetence of your people?
72. Does your management style with any given subordinate stay constant if you manage him over a long period of time?
73. Do you discuss your department's mistakes with other departments?
74. Do you produce notes and systems to help less experienced people with tasks?

75. Do you feel valued at work?
76. Are you too busy to teach people how to do the job?
77. Do you look forward to quite a lot of aspects of your work?
78. Do you enjoy influencing?
79. Do you think that if the company got recruitment right it wouldn't be necessary to coach people?
80. Do you enjoy having privileged information?

If the answer you gave corresponds to the answer in the box opposite the relevant question number, then you score 1 point in the column the letter is under. So, for example, if you answered 'yes' to question 1, score 1 point under 'coaching'. You can remember by putting a cross in that box, or shading it in. At the end, count up how many shaded boxes you have in each column (the maximum in any column is 20).

	D	Coa	V	Con
1		Y		
2	Y			
3		Y		
4		Y		
5	N			
6		N		
7			N	
8	N			
9				Y
10	N			
11			Y	
12		Y		
13				N
14	Y			
15	N			
16			Y	
17		Y		
18				Y
19	N			
20		N		

	D	Coa	V	Con
41		N		
42			Y	
43	N			
44		N		
45	Y			
46				Y
47			Y	
48		N		
49				N
50			Y	
51	Y			
52		Y		
53			Y	
54				N
55	Y			
56				N
57			N	
58	N			
59				Y
60			Y	

	D	Coa	V	Con
21			N	
22				Y
23	Y			
24		Y		
25				N
26			N	
27			Y	
28	Y			
29				Y
30			Y	
31		Y		
32				N
33			N	
34				N
35	Y			
36				Y
37	N			
38			Y	
39			Y	
40		Y		

	D	Coa	V	Con
61				N
62	N			
63				N
64			N	
65		Y		
66		Y		
67	N			
68				N
69			Y	
70	N			
71				N
72		N		
73				Y
74		Y		
75				Y
76		N		
77			Y	
78			Y	
79		N		
80	N			

You now have a rough guide on the extent to which you are likely to be a disclosing, coaching, visioning and confident developer of change agents. The nearer 20 you have scored on any scale, the more indications there are that you behave in that way.

You will also be able to see which is already your area of greatest strength and which area you need to develop in.

Let's look now at some ideas to help you develop in each of the four key areas.

How to disclose more

- Ask your people whether they feel they get enough information from you. What else would they like to know?

- Ask yourself, continually, whether there are things about the organization which you could be telling this person which would make more sense of his task or interest and enthuse him or enable him to contribute more?
- If you're genuinely worried you might disclose too much, check with your boss. But at some point you will have to make your own judgements.
- Create more opportunities to talk and, more importantly, to be asked questions. These can range from actual meetings (expensive in people's time and sometimes an inappropriate forum for open discussion) to 'management by walking about'.
- Start a noticeboard or a newsletter.
- Make sure you give people more rather than less information than they've asked for when they ask you a question.
- Say 'I don't know' if you don't, and don't worry about it. You are not expected to have all the answers.
- Ask other people what they think: 'I believe this is what's going on, but how does it look to you?'

How to coach more

You may actually need to be coached in coaching! Coaching requires a quite specific set of skills, including: skill at diagnosing people's level of competence and what the blocks to their competence are; skill at asking them questions which encourage them to explore and develop solutions to problems; skill at giving them feedback on what they have done well and what less well; skill at keeping the right amount of control over their activities while they are learning. There are courses, books and videos on coaching skills, but best of all is to find yourself a role model, someone whom you consider to be an excellent coach, and watch!

The key to coaching, however, is to ask your people how they would tackle assignments rather than to launch into telling them how to. Be prepared to recognize their ideas as better. If you ask expecting a specific reply which must correspond with the plan in your head, then you are not coaching, simply playing 'guess and tell'!

Ask yourself whether there are things you are currently doing which you could delegate, if you just spent a bit of time coaching. I know a managing director who spent an average of four hours a week over two months coaching a quite junior assistant in doing the company books. It was a heavy investment at the time, but the firm's accounting bills have been vastly reduced. The coaching manager is alert to the potential of people for enlarging their areas of responsibility all the time.

How to vision more

- Ask yourself the following questions: How would I like things to be different? Where could we be more successful? What untapped potential do we have?
- Make a habit of looking for the pay-offs and the benefits in courses of action.
- Go to art classes.
- Read books by people who get excited about change and organizational issues (Tom Peters, Rosabeth Moss Kanter, John Harvey-Jones, to name just three).
- Abandon cynicism. It's a self-fulfilling prophecy, and a managerial cop-out.
- Don't ever try to vision in someone else's style. And don't have the idea that you have to use literary or flowery phrases. It's your own conviction that matters.
- Get involved. If you stay on the sidelines of change, watching it, appraising it, you won't connect enough with it to vision.

How to be more confident

- Sort out your relationship with your boss. Establish your value, your constraints, your freedoms, your accountabilities. Get clarity.
- Achieve the things which are important to your own job security and success.

- Avoid paranoid organizations and people – if you are lacking in confidence, these will wear you right down.
- Understand that you are not indispensable, nor should you be. I recently heard the managing director of an organization say to his senior staff that their first responsibility was to make themselves dispensable.
- Understand that your value does not depend on your being better than everyone around you, but rather on you and them combined being better than the competition.

Conclusion

I hope that the picture I have painted of the kind of people who will breed the next generation of change agents does not sound impossibly idealistic. I have met many, many individuals, at all organizational levels, who have all these qualities and more.

8

Secure in Change:
How to Progress Your Career

Farewell to job security

In a book about change, we have to acknowledge that many organizations change by getting smaller, and many that do and don't change cease to exist. Not only that, but as organizations adjust their portfolio of competence and track the market's demands, they will inevitably engage in a continuous process of adjusting their people resource.

So for most of us this era of change is going to mean – indeed, already means – more job changes, some chosen, some enforced. Far fewer of us can now feel we have a 'job for life', and the days when employers encouraged a 'cradle to grave' attitude towards employees are largely gone.

If we had simply lost job security, with nothing to replace it, we should all be feeling pretty despondent about this. After all, many of the preceding chapters have stressed the importance of high self-esteem and robust self-confidence in dealing with change, and the fear of losing one's job saps both of those.

There is, however, something with which we can replace job security, and it is something which will make us even keener to welcome change and learn from the new experiences change inevitably brings in train. It is something I shall call 'ability security'. It might also be called 'marketability security', but that label perhaps makes it sound narrower than it should.

Ability security is the security which derives from your knowledge that you can do things. It increases when you develop new skills, or acquire new experiences which mean you can apply your skills to a wider range of situations; it increases when you add to your knowledge; it increases when you remove blocks to your competence, such as anxiety or a tendency to lose your temper. Unlike job security, which has always been very much determined by others – by the people running the company, by the government, or by the shareholders – ability security is very much within our own control. I can increase my ability security by learning a foreign language or taking an MBA, for example.

Also, ability security cannot be taken away from you. Nor is it reduced when you change jobs. In fact, it is generally increased, because you will inevitably develop new areas of competence in a new job, and you won't lose the ones you already have. Whereas too much emphasis on job security encourages us to stay put and to fear organizational change, shifting the emphasis to ability security encourages us to move around and to welcome organizational change as providing us with opportunities to grow. Even being made redundant can result in an increase in ability security: the very experience of redundancy, if we manage it right, will make us more resilient, more resourceful, more knowledgeable about the job market, and so on.

All of this makes ability security sound a very attractive concept, but of course it does have a potential drawback when compared with job security. There is a certain tangibility to job security, expressed most clearly in the words of our contract; in contrast, ability security sounds rather vague. Of course, the tangibility of job security often turns out to be more of a mirage that it suits us all to pretend to believe in; nevertheless, job security can be defined and bounded, and that is reassuring.

So, in order to make ability security just as potentially reassuring, we need a way to make it less abstract, more concrete. We need a way to describe our ability security at any one time and to track whether it is increasing or decreasing.

The way is via our curriculum vitae (CV). But not via the typical list of educational experiences, qualifications, and positions held. (In fact, even the typical CV has come on a long way in recent years. The fundamental change is that people are seeing it less and less as a factual record, more and more as a 'selling document'. If you are interested in the basic principles of a good modern CV, you might like to read *The Right Way to Write Your Own CV* by John Clarke (Paperfronts 1989).) To do your ability security justice, you will need to expand your vision of what a CV is even further.

Managing your CV

So we are going to place emphasis on 'managing' your CV. This is not the same as simply compiling it, or keeping it up to date – it is more than this. Managing your CV entails investing in particular experiences, making active choices, in order to produce a CV with a set of characteristics you identify in advance as being the ones you want; it also entails describing the consequences of those experiences and choices in a way you have designed to produce a particular effect on the reader.

When prospective employers ask for a CV, they are usually expecting a fairly chronological record of your relevant experience. I say 'fairly chronological' because it is quite acceptable to produce the record with the most recent experience first – that is, reverse chronological – in order to highlight the importance of the most relevant entries; it is also becoming more and more common for people to pull out themes and certain personal and/or professional strengths in their chronological CVs. To illustrate these points, there follows an example of what I would call a fairly enlightened chronological CV:

Barbara Jenkins MA: Curriculum Vitae

An impeccable academic record including a First Class Degree from Oxford University. Spent six years as a teacher and as an educational psychologist before moving to a systems consultancy. Now runs a team of consultants engaged in state-of-the-art operational research on decision-making. Author of a textbook on psychology in schools. She effectively packages her very significant skills, and her expertise lies anywhere that requires intellect, integrity and determination.

PERSONAL DETAILS

Barbara Jenkins   born 8th May 1955

12 Bulmershe Road, Strettingham

0702–391384

British

Graduate Member of the ACP

Accredited administrator of psychological tests.

EDUCATION

1966–1973	City of Worcester Grammar School for Girls. 8 O levels (six at Grade 1) 3 A levels (English, French and German, all Grade A) 1 S level with distinction (French)
1974–1977	St Hilda's College, University of Oxford. Scholarship for distinction in Preliminary Examinations BA (Hons) First Class in Experimental Psychology
1977–1978	Education Department, University of Oxford Postgraduate Certificate in Education, with Distinction
1984	O level Physics (Grade A)

EMPLOYMENT

1978–1980	Teacher of English, and Remedial Education Specialist, at Graham Abbey Upper School, Oxford
1980–1984	Psychologist with Oxfordshire Local Education Authority.
1985 to the present	Consultant, then Senior Consultant, with

Human Computer Interfaces Limited, 3 The
Mews, Stanton, Gloucestershire.

PUBLICATIONS

Jenkins, B., 'Decisions on Decision Aids'. Proceedings Human
Behaviour Symposium, Wembley, England, 1987.
Jenkins, B., 'Methods and Approaches for Psychology Teaching
in Schools', Burbon Press, London, 1989.

INTERESTS

Reading, professional writing, bridge, tennis, and croquet.
Speaking and reading French and German. Entertaining and
debating. Member of the Parish Church Council. Member of the
village singing group.

CAREER HISTORY

Barbara Jenkins achieved outstanding qualifications during her
secondary education, and won a place at St Hilda's College,
Oxford, to study Experimental Psychology. There, she was
awarded a Scholarship for success in Preliminary Examinations,
and subsequently confirmed that promise by achieving a First
Class Degree.

Barbara then decided to follow a career in education, and
gained a Postgraduate Certificate in Education, with Distinction,
from Oxford University. Her first teaching post was as a teacher
of English at a secondary school in Oxford, and there she
broadened her skills to become a qualified Specialist in Remedial
Education.

Wishing to pursue both Remedial Education and her qualification in Psychology, Barbara moved after two years to become a
Psychologist with Oxfordshire Local Education Authority. Her
work involved interviewing teachers and families, assessing
children of all ages, conducting family therapy, and contributing
to the training of less specialized teachers. In the course of this
work Barbara gained particular skills in professional interviewing and counselling, in running effective group sessions, and in
the administration and use of standard psychological tests.

In 1985, cutbacks in the Education Service convinced Barbara that she should seek a different career. After considering a number of opportunities, she joined Human Computer Interfaces Limited. HCI is a small and prestigious systems consultancy with a niche market in user-centred systems design, operational research and advanced computing.

At HCI, Barbara first joined a team of consultants providing technical and programme advice to the project manager of a large finance-related computer system then under development. She was involved in documenting the design, participating in design reviews, and working with a mixed technical and client team to assess the organizational and work impacts of the system.

In 1987, Barbara joined an HCI team undertaking operational analysis of decision-making in the stock exchange. She now leads this team of five consultants, whose task is to diagnose and report on functional and dysfunctional decision-making behaviour during dealing crises. Her team deals with strategy, procedure and creativity as observed not only in single decision-makers, but also in the associated organizational network.

In addition to being the final technical arbiter of her team's work, Barbara handles the contractual aspects of the project, and undertakes personal management of the individuals in her team, particularly advising on their career development within the company.

Barbara's wider responsibilities within HCI are for marketing and proposal writing in relevant areas of the company's business. She also contributes to the company's recruitment activities by interviewing and administering tests to applicants. She has formalized the company's test procedures, and has introduced a standardized test which taps effectively those skills most relevant to the company's operations.

In addition to her work with HCI, Barbara has written a textbook on psychology for schools. She wanted to make her insights and knowledge available on a more widespread basis, and to package them in a form suitable for the school market. Not only has Barbara's book found an enthusiastic publisher, but she has single-handedly managed the necessary interactions with agents, editors and publicists in seeing the book through to publication. She has participated in an extensive publicity tour of local radio stations, and has been interviewed for a variety of consumer affairs and magazine programmes.

In summary, Barbara Jenkins's successful career is the demonstration of her remarkable intellect, clarity of thought and determination, coupled with a talent for communication and dealing with people at all levels.

The chronological CV is an important concrete manifestation of your 'ability'. It demonstrates what you know, what you have done, and, by implication, what you can do.

In using your chronological CV to maximize your ability security, there are some useful principles to follow:

- Group qualifications in a way which makes it crystal clear what the underlying skill(s) are which the qualifications are evidence of. For example:

  Languages   A-level French and German

                       Diploma in Business French

  Computer skills   Certificate of competence in D Base II

                       HND in Computing Studies

- Include details of activities which have led to the development of a skill but did not lead to a formal qualification. For example:

  Languages   French conversation classes attended weekly for two years. Employs French au pair to look after children and keep family conversational French up to scratch.

- When identifying a particular work experience, make clear the nature of what you were actually doing and therefore of the skill(s) you were exercising. Make sure you don't assume people will automatically understand all the job involves.

Make sure you differentiate the particularly challenging aspects of your role. For example, don't write 'Project manager, Weston Green Enterprises'; write instead:

Project manager, large (15) team of mixed specialisms. Liaison and integration between different functional specialisms a particular responsibility.

- To help you do the above, ask yourself, for each piece of work experience: What made this job difficult/challenging? What made the job interesting? Why was I good/bad at it?
- In your 'base' chronological CV – that is, the one you keep on file and draw from when you are submitting a specific CV to a potential employer – include *everything* you've done! Also, in addition to keeping it as up to date as you can, review the whole CV every six months or so. When you have some distance from a previous job, you can often see better how you developed, what you learned, and what skills you exercised in that job. Such insights enable you to write a much more compelling entry on your CV.

The key thing to remember is that your chronological CV is not a historical document; it is an assessment of your potential value to an employer. It is the certificate of your 'ability', and the most tangible expression of your ability security.

It will help you construct a chronological CV which really serves this purpose if you also develop what I shall call your 'conceptual' CV.

The conceptual CV

A conceptual CV is a model of your professional competence. Because there may be more than one model of competence which fits you at any point in time, you can have several conceptual CVs.

The conceptual CV is not sent to an employer. It can therefore take many forms, and you should feel free to be creative in developing your own models of competence, and in depicting them in whatever way means most to you.

What you do in a conceptual CV is to identify areas of skill or competence which you possess. You also identify the 'evidence' you have that you possess these skills, and you look for patterns, links and gaps in the picture which emerges.

I might for example identify my two main areas of competence as being electrical engineering and departmental management. I might draw the 'model' like this:

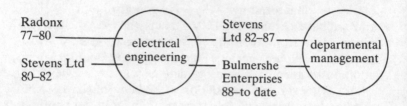

This might prompt me to consider whether it was time to get some experience of departmental management in a field un-related to electrical engineering. This would increase the breadth of my competence – and hence my ability security – markedly.

Here are some more examples of parts of conceptual CVs.

Example 1

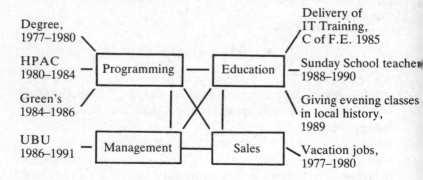

Example 1 shows an individual who has identified four main skill areas which he feels he possesses: programming, education, management, sales. He has briefly summarized the evidence for his possessing each of the skill areas.

This conceptual CV highlights the nature of his breadth of skills in a way a chronological CV would not have done, and it enables him to look for ways he could combine different skill areas to pursue different kinds of job opportunity. He might look to capitalize on the interplay between programming, sales and management by seeking a senior sales executive position in an information technology company, for example.

The conceptual CV also highlights an interest and area of skill he has not yet capitalized on in his formal career, 'education'. This opens up new avenues of possibility.

Example 2

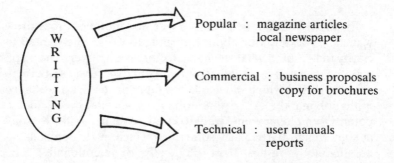

Example 2 shows part of a conceptual CV in which the individual concerned gets to grips with the nature and extent of her writing skill. She had never had a job which had formally demanded writing skills, but realized that she had often ended up writing for significant parts of her day. She was considering a career change, and wondering whether this might indicate a direction.

Example 3

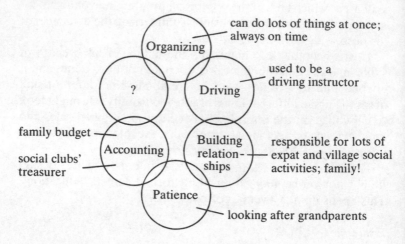

Example 3 shows the picture a wife and mother of four drew when she was thinking about returning to work. She wanted to clarify in her mind what she had to offer an employer. The circle with the question mark indicates her feeling there was something missing – a gap which she needed to fill to have a serious chance in the job market. After pondering it for a while, she decided a potential employer would want to know about her ability to 'stick at something', particularly something which made demands on her mentally rather than physically or emotionally. The 'accounting' skill was relevant here, but she felt she needed to bolster her ability profile a bit. She decided to enrol for an evening class in A-level English.

Example 3 shows how the conceptual CV highlights imbalances and gaps, and raises questions such as:

- Is my competence concentrated too much in one area?
- Is there something obvious missing?
- Can I significantly increase my ability security by adding a particular new kind of experience?

It doesn't matter what pictures, shapes and words you use for your conceptual CV. What is important is that it enables you to assess your ability security and to plan how to improve it.

The conceptual CVs we have looked at are based around the idea of skills. They might also be based around other key ideas in any assessment of our value in employment terms. One such is the idea of 'domains of contact' or, more strongly, 'domains of influence'. What kinds of people do you know? With what kinds of people have you worked? Who have you demonstrated you can communicate with? Work with? Influence?

You might, for example, decide that 'educating' was one of your skills. Now think comprehensively about all the contexts in which you have 'educated' others. Clearly, fifteen years of success educating pupils in maths at a grammar school is evidence of a different kind of ability from five years of educating a mixed bunch of local youngsters in natural history, giving talks on Japan to a range of local social clubs, and working as a part-time driving instructor. It's not just different because of the different content; much more importantly, it's different because the nature of the educational challenge is different. The demands are different, and so the skills they elicit from you are different.

Perhaps I can illustrate the power of the conceptual CV over the straightforward and traditional chronological CV with a true story about two friends of mine. Both these friends – let's call them Joe and David – wanted ultimately to gain academic posts in modern languages as lecturers or research fellows, in a redbrick university. They had this ambition at a time when universities were decreasing their staff, and competition for any post was ferocious. Neither could hope to walk straight into academia on completion of his doctorate.

Joe decided to build experience and skill in education and modern languages. For him, the conceptual CV was paramount. He was going to add relevant skills and experiences until his ability security was so impressive he would be able to win the kind of job to which he aspired.

Joe took any opportunity available to educate and research in French and German. He taught at European literature summer schools in Britain and the USA; he gave evening classes in rough areas of London, where the challenge was to get across Romantic French poetry to a bunch of largely hostile teenagers; he taught for several terms in schools; he took part-time jobs in any college or polytechnic which offered. Not only was he developing his skills as an educator, but he was making contacts all the time. Joe made sure he did not loose touch with his academic contacts, but he added to them.

After five years, he got his first full-time post at a university. Now, after ten years, he is a senior lecturer at one of the best university modern language departments in the UK.

David, in contrast, focused much more on trying to move along the typical track leading to an academic appointment in a redbrick university. He kept trying for research and lecturing vacancies in universities; because there weren't many vacancies, he had to wait a long time before he got his first opportunity: eight hours of modern language coaching a week at Oxford University. He has, over three years, managed to increase this to fifteen hours a week during term time, but he still has no permanent job, nor any firm prospect of one.

What kept Joe motivated all the time he was doing things so different from what he really wanted to do was his conceptual CV. He knew he was growing all the time in skill and experience as an educator in his chosen field; and he was confident that he would be able to turn all of this into an irresistible chronological CV at some point in the future. This made him positive, opportunistic and busy. In fact, even if Joe had never managed to get a university appointment, he would probably have found many other possibilities to interest him on the way.

This raises another important point about conceptual CVs. The act of constructing a conceptual CV encourages us to think broadly about our competence, and to develop our abilities down many different paths rather than along one narrow track. And, as you will remember from earlier in this book, *range* of ability is important if we are to respond flexibly and positively to change.

How can you get started on your conceptual CV? Here are a few tips.

- Take a blank sheet of paper and brainstorm all the skills, qualities and positive characteristics you think you have. Then start drawing connections between these, to build them into clusters of related abilities.
- Ask a friend to interview you on the subject of 'What are you good at? And how do you know?'. Tape-record the interview and use it as a basis for starting your conceptual CV.
- Take one or more of the multitude of 'competency models' in management texts. Identify which of the competencies you have, and why. Think about filling the gaps.
- Walk yourself mentally through a typical day. Jot down every time you do something which is evidence of a different ability. Remember that your conceptual CV doesn't have to be neat or logical – it just has to mean something to you.

Removing blocks

Before we leave the explanation of the 'conceptual CV', we ought to remind ourselves of the power of removing blocks to ability security as well as of adding skills. Right at the beginning of this chapter we mentioned in passing the fact that ability security increases when you remove the blocks to competence, such as anxiety. Let's think a little more about this.

You may draw up your conceptual CV and be mystified that you still don't feel confident and you still are not professionally successful. Perhaps you have a large number of skills, and considerable experience, but you know in your heart of hearts that if you lost your current job you wouldn't find another one easily.

In this case, it is likely that somewhere there are one or more blocks to the expression of your underlying competence. I know, for example, a highly qualified, highly skilled individual who is not at all flexible in terms of the context in which she can work. She has a very bad temper, and there aren't many organizations

105

which are prepared to tolerate her outbursts. She has found an environment where the quality of her research means that people turn a blind eye to her temper tantrums; but she won't get promoted, and there are few industrial organizations which would risk employing her. Clearly, there is one priority she must address above all others if she is to increase her ability security. It makes little sense for her to add new skills to her conceptual CV while it contains such an enormous block.

Blocks, in the sense I am using the word here, are emotional patterns or personality characteristics which get in the way of your making maximum use of your knowledge, skills and experience. A block may be as obvious as a stammer or as complex as resentment of authority figures. It is often blocks like these which set the limits to a person's effectiveness at work, far more than lack of knowledge or skill. Although only the most skilful of interviewers and sophisticated of assessment procedures will show up these blocks when you apply for a job, it is worth doing something about them. Removing one or more will be a major boost to your confidence, and that will communicate itself in every interview you go to.

How to remove them is a topic beyond the scope of this book. You might like to delve a bit deeper into removing blocks to personal effectiveness, explored in my earlier book, *How to Get Things Done* (Sheldon 1990); or you might want to see how counselling or therapy could help.

The key message here is that when you draw up your conceptual CV you should ask yourself whether you express your competence effectively in all contexts. There may be blocks in there, too, which either lower your ability across the board or compromise it in specific situations.

Ability security and career choices

Switching from the notion of job security to that of ability security has quite an impact on some of the 'conventional wisdom' when it comes to career choices.

For example, it leads us to redefine what a 'dead-end job' is.

Traditionally, a dead-end job is one from which you'll never be promoted. But we should redefine it as one which does not progress your conceptual CV. So the opportunity to fast-track 'up the management ladder' could be 'dead-end' for you, if what you really need, to increase your ability security, is greater breadth of experience in operations. And a lateral move, far from being a delay, might be just what you need to plug a gap on your conceptual CV and become really 'ability secure'.

In fact, you can see that in many ways the faster the rise, the more precarious you become, and now that job security is largely gone, you could pay a high price for that precariousness. One senior executive I know has fast-tracked to director level without having acquired any man-management experience. There's a big hole in her conceptual CV, although her chronological CV looks impressive.

Another consequence of adopting the notion of 'ability security' is that gaps in your chronological CV are no longer such a disaster. For the fact that you took a break from conventional employment does not necessarily mean you took a break from developing your conceptual CV. And people who have adapted to being without paid work often have a much broader range of response than people who have been in paid work continuously. You do need to be careful how you represent gaps on your chronological CV, since recruiters are still taught to regard them as danger signs. But as our understanding grows of which kinds of experience equip people best to adapt to change, such 'gaps' will be seen more and more as positive rather than negative indicators.

Perhaps the most fundamental shift in emphasis which the shift from job security to ability security brings is the one related to the nature of the emotional contract between employer and employee. Whereas job security implies 'I'll work hard for you if you'll look after me', ability security implies 'I'll increase your marketability if you'll increase mine'. And this means that what we all need to place greatest emphasis on whenever we are thinking of taking a new job is the capacity of this new job to progress our conceptual CV. If we will simply be doing exactly what we have done before, but for more money, we should think again. If the job offers significant development opportunity, challenges us in new ways, or, best of all, plugs a specific gap in our ability profile, then these are strong arguments in favour of taking it.

Marketability

We've mentioned 'marketability' a few times now, and given all that's been said above, it's a concept we all need to have at the forefront of our minds as we develop our careers. In a way, we each need a personal 'marketability barometer' which tells us whether our marketability is rising or falling.

So how do you assess your marketability?

- Apply for jobs and see if you get interviews.
- Study the jobs advertisements in the papers and check them out against your own conceptual CV.
- Read, listen, and talk all the time to discover which skills are currently most valued, which declining in value, which 'flavour of the month'.
- Try to keep a mental list of 'other jobs' you could currently do.
- Notice among your colleagues, friends and acquaintances who get new jobs easily and who do not.
- Observe the extent to which you have advice and comment to offer, which people find useful, in a whole range of situations.

Many new jobs will start off by decreasing your marketability (few other organizations will want to employ you if you left your last job too soon); then they increase it (you acquire new skills and experience); and then they begin to decrease it again (you run the risk of being typecast, or getting set in your ways). You need to be sensitive to the point at which your job begins to decrease your marketability and do something. You don't have to leave; you can start doing your job in a different way, expand your role, identify someone in the organization you can learn something new from, ask for formal development activity.

The key lies in your conceptual CV. If you've had nothing to add for six months, it's likely you're on the down-slope of the marketability curve.

Ultimately, your marketability depends on the extent to which potential employers see your ability profile as matching the profile of their vacancy. So when it comes to producing a CV for a specific job – drawing on your base chronological CV and your conceptual CV – you need to emphasize aspects which are relevant to that job. This exercise not only increases your chances of getting the job; it also encourages you to see your personal resources as something which can be adapted and moulded to fit different situations. In short, it encourages you to see yourself as someone who can respond positively to change, who is not limited by past experience and particular expertise, who is not restricted to doing the same things over and over again. In fact, the exercise is so helpful as a means of building a change-agent approach to your own career that it is worth doing even when you're not actually going to send off the CVs.

If you find that the idea of a conceptual CV appeals to you, you can read more about how to see yourself and your competence in new ways in *What Color is Your Parachute?* by Richard Nelson Bolles (Ten Speed Press 1992).

Conclusion

Change is frightening, and it's exciting. Whether it works for good or ill has a lot to do with how we meet it. Now that you have read this book I hope you feel better equipped to provoke it, use it, make it happen on *your* terms; I hope too you are beginning to think about how things could be different, and better, in your workplace.

Organizations depend for their survival on that kind of individual initiative and courage. Yet, as we have discussed and explored in this book, the vast majority of organizations are, in their basic systems and assumptions, inimical to change agents.

So you will have a fight on your hands. A fight not only against your own anxieties, but against the creaking organizational structures which resist movement and spontaneity. The only answer is to enjoy the fight, just as you should enjoy wrestling with change. Experiment with your creativity; wield your influence; stir up placid and complacent groups; and, above all, develop yourself and the next generation of change agents.

Index